1 2 3 4 5 6 7 8 9 10

THE TECH SET

Ellyssa Kroski, Series Editor

WITHDRAWN

Next-Gen Library Catalogs

Marshall Breeding

Neal-Schuman Publishers, Inc.

New York   London

Published by Neal-Schuman Publishers, Inc.
100 William St., Suite 2004
New York, NY 10038

Published in cooperation with the Library Information and Technology Association, a division of the American Library Association.

Printed and bound in the United States of America.

The paper used in this publication meets the minimum requirements of American National Standard for Information Sciences—Permanence of Paper for Printed Library Materials, ANSI Z39.48-1992.

ISBN: 978-1-55570-708-8

This book is dedicated to Zora,
my wife, colleague, constant companion, and best friend.

CONTENTS

Don't miss this book's companion wiki and podcast!

Turn the page for details.

THE TECH SET is more than the book you're holding!

All 10 titles in THE TECH SET series feature three components:

1. the book you're now holding;
2. companion wikis to provide even more details on the topic and keep our coverage of this topic up-to-date; and
3. author podcasts that will extend your knowledge and let you get to know the author even better.

The companion wikis and podcasts can be found at:

techset.wetpaint.com

At **techset.wetpaint.com** you'll be able to go far beyond the printed pages you're now holding and:

- ▶ access regular updates from each author that are packed with new advice and recommended resources;
- ▶ use the wiki's forum to interact, ask questions, and share advice with the authors and your LIS peers; and
- ▶ hear these gurus' own words when you listen to THE TECH SET podcasts.

To receive regular updates about TECH SET technologies and authors, sign up for THE TECH SET Facebook page (**facebook.com/ nealschumanpub**) and Twitter (**twitter.com/nealschumanpub**).

For more information on THE TECH SET series and the individual titles, visit **www.neal-schuman.com/techset**.

▶

FOREWORD

Welcome to volume 1 of The Tech Set.

Next-Gen Library Catalogs is an all-in-one passport to today's cutting-edge library catalogs that incorporate social features and encourage patron participation. The authority on library automation trends and technology, Marshall Breeding gives a complete overview of what options libraries have available to them for adding 2.0 features such as personalization, patron ratings and reviews, faceted navigation, and related resources recommendations to their catalogs. This exceptional practical volume walks the reader through how to integrate a discovery interface with the ILS, including how to extract ILS data, integrate article-level content, establish real-time interactions, and more.

The idea for The Tech Set book series developed because I perceived a need for a set of practical guidebooks for using today's cutting-edge technologies specifically within libraries. When I give talks and teach courses, what I hear most from librarians who are interested in implementing these new tools in their organizations are questions on how exactly to go about doing it. A lot has been written about the benefits of these new 2.0 social media tools, and at this point librarians are intrigued but they oftentimes don't know where to start.

I envisioned a series of books that would offer accessible, practical information and would encapsulate the spirit of a 23 Things program but go a step further—to teach librarians not only how to use these programs as individual users but also how to plan and implement particular types of library services using them. I thought it was important to discuss the entire life cycle of these initiatives, including everything from what it takes to plan, strategize, and gain buy-in, to how to develop and implement, to how to market and measure the success of these projects. I also wanted them to incorporate a broad range of project ideas and instructions.

Each of the ten books in The Tech Set series was written with this format in mind. Throughout the series, the "Implementation" chapters, chock-full of detailed project instructions, will be of major interest to all readers. These chapters start off with a basic "recipe" for how to effectively use the technology in a library, and then build on that foundation to offer more and more advanced project ideas. I believe that readers of all levels of expertise will find something useful here as the proposed projects and initiatives run the gamut from the basic to the cutting-edge.

I have had the pleasure of hearing Marshall Breeding speak at numerous library conferences and have consulted his prolific writings on library automation many times. Marshall is one of those professionals who can encapsulate his decades of experience and expertise in a way that is completely accessible to his audience. And that is exactly what he has achieved with *Next-Gen Library Catalogs*, a comprehensible guidebook to today's social catalogs. If you want to learn what's involved with adopting this type of technology in your library, this is a must-read resource.

Ellyssa Kroski
Information Services Technologist
Barnard College Library
www.ellyssakroski.com
http://oedb.org/blogs/ilibrarian
ellyssakroski@yahoo.com

Ellyssa Kroski is an Information Services Technologist at Barnard College as well as a writer, educator, and international conference speaker. She is an adjunct faculty member at Long Island University, Pratt Institute, and San Jose State University where she teaches LIS students about emerging technologies. Her book *Web 2.0 for Librarians and Information Professionals* was published in February 2008, and she is the creator and Series Editor for The Tech Set 10-volume book series. She blogs at iLibrarian and writes a column called "Stacking the Tech" for *Library Journal*'s Academic Newswire.

PREFACE

In an age when most people usually begin and end every search with Google, the conventional online library catalog seems just about as obsolete a concept as its predecessor, the card catalog. To stay relevant, today's libraries need to offer an Internet search presence that blends Web 2.0 technologies with library-centered content, one that enables users to quickly reach the rich multimedia collections found within both digital and physical collections.

Next-gen library catalogs do just that. They connect users with books, videos, articles, photographs, and other library content via new Web 2.0 discovery interface services.

▶ ORGANIZATION AND AUDIENCE

Because many librarians (like most library users) have never encountered a real next-gen catalog, *Next-Gen Library Catalogs* has been designed to be readable by nontechnical staff members, systems librarians, network and computer administrators, and other technical staff, all who will benefit from its description of the many uses. Library administrators in all types of settings will find information here that can enable them to make more informed decisions regarding new products for their library. Staff working in settings with higher proportions of digital content will find useful information on how to manage a complex collection. Public and school libraries that have implemented a next-gen catalog already enjoy increasing levels of circulation, benefitting from information that will help them manage their growing electronic resources collections.

In the pages that follow, Chapter 1 sets the stage, looking at why libraries need to adopt Web-based discovery interfaces and proactively keep abreast of new search technologies. Chapter 2 then details what's different about this new genre of interfaces. Chapter 3 covers implementation of new next-gen catalog services and features a quick tour of emerging products.

Once a library chooses and implements a new interface to its collection, it's time to market it. Chapter 4 provides details on marketing to the public and on winning the support of fellow staff members. Chapter 5 covers next-gen catalog best practices and provides tips for maximum usefulness; Chapter 6 looks at Web analytics and other reporting tools for measuring not only the interface's activity level but also its use patterns across the total collection.

After reading *Next-Gen Library Catalogs*, staff members from the technical services to the reference departments should have new ideas about how to use this exciting new interface in day-to-day services. These new tools can—with the same amount of resource investment—allow every library to provide users with the most efficient access possible to the total spectrum of the library's physical and digital resources.

INTRODUCTION: NEXT-GEN LIBRARY CATALOG BASICS

► **Terminology**
► **Evolution of Library Catalogs**
► **The Status Quo: Legacy Online Catalogs**

The movement toward a new generation of library catalogs represents one of the most important technology-based transitions libraries currently face. A major portion of the interactions between a library and its users takes place through its Web site and its online catalog. When it comes to facilities for providing services to its users, the library's Web site ranks second only to its physical premises. Given the Web site's prominence, it is vital that libraries do all that they can to deliver services on the Web in a way that meets or exceeds expectations. This book explores the realm of new discovery interfaces and their role in delivering access to content and providing services to library users. We'll examine the approaches that have been in place in the recent past and provide a more modern approach with the alternatives that are emerging.

Unfortunately, in recent years libraries have lagged behind other Web destinations in the way that they deliver their services and provide access to their collections. Though this statement makes a sweeping generalization, it reflects a broad trend in the realm of library automation that can be supported by comparing typical library Web sites with popular Web sites. We're seeing a generational change in the products available to libraries for their online catalogs, which hopefully will provide a more modern approach to this key component of the library's Web presence.

This introductory chapter attempts to identify some of the short-comings associated with the current state of affairs, where most libraries rely on the online catalog module delivered with their automation system as their primary search interface. We'll place this into the perspective of the progressive development of the Web and describe how the older generation library catalogs compare in the context of today's Web experience. Yet hope is not lost. A new generation of products are emerging that stand to help libraries compete in this era when our users bring tremendously heightened expectations for the delivery of information on the Web.

▶ TERMINOLOGY

The products we'll be talking about throughout this book defy labels. The newer ways of approaching what goes on within a library differ quite a bit from what came before, but the old names persist. Let's review some of the terminology that we'll be using throughout this book.

The **online catalog**, also known as the Online Public Access Catalog (OPAC), is the interface component of an integrated library system (ILS). Its features allow library users to search the resources managed within the ILS. Online catalogs typically allow library users to perform self-service requests on items displayed, such as placing holds and renewing items previously charged.

We've grown accustomed to the term "catalog," but it is not necessarily a term that library users understand without explanation, especially with regard to what is or is not included. Libraries depend on their **integrated library system** to automate the basic operations of the library, including acquiring, describing, and providing access to the items in their collections. While these systems differ in many ways, they tend to follow similar groupings in how they deliver their functionality. The cataloging module provides tools for describing resources, acquisitions deals with the procurement of items (ordering, payment, managing funds), circulation manages the processes involved in loaning materials to library users, and the online catalog provides an interface for library users to search the resources managed by the ILS.

A new genre of software has emerged that aims to replace the traditional online catalog. So what do we call these products that are emerging that involve providing access to library collections and services in some new ways? These products tend to be called **next-generation library catalogs**, although this terminology doesn't exactly capture the essence of the genre. The word "catalog" isn't especially helpful in describing this category of products. While we'll talk later about the specific features and concepts addressed by these emerging products, generally they aim to modernize the interface and expand the scope beyond what was possible with the earlier products. The online catalogs were delivered as a component of the ILS. These new products don't have the same relation with the library's automation environment; they usually address a broader set of content than what is managed by the ILS. This new breed of software focuses on providing access to the broad set of resources that comprise library collections.

This broader scope of search aims to help library users find resources managed in multiple systems, including content to which a library subscribes from external providers. These products aim to help library users discover the resources available among the many different aspects of a library's collections and to manage the process of making that resource available for them. This broader function has led to the term **discovery interfaces**.

These new products break away from the established mold and introduce a whole cluster of new features: a more modern, Web-savvy interface; access to social networks; and a broader approach to discovering and exploring library collections. Discovery interfaces incorporate the newer tools and concepts to which users are becoming accustomed—such as tagging, integrated social features, easy search, intuitive navigation, and relevancy-ranked results—into more effective searches of the high-quality content supplied by the library.

▶ EVOLUTION OF LIBRARY CATALOGS

One of the most vital services of libraries is providing access to their collections. The concept of the catalog has been part of libraries since their earliest history. The collections that libraries build are of little value without tools that help readers discover items of interest. Catalogs serve as vehicles of discovery into library collections.

Each generation of library has created tools using the approach appropriate for its time. From the ancient past through current times, libraries have used the technologies drawn from broader society to organize and provide access to their collections. In recent times, the cycles of technology have turned very quickly, making it difficult for libraries to stay ahead of the curve.

As I have visited some historic libraries, it's fascinating to see some of the original catalogs used to record the holdings of the library, often handwritten bound volumes. These catalogs provided a register of the books in a collection but had many limitations. Prior to automation, most libraries maintained card catalogs to help users find materials. Card catalogs were the status quo when I began working in libraries. These catalogs relied on multiple cards for each work, providing multiple points of access, including author, title, and subjects.

As computers entered the scene, libraries were anxious to automate their circulation operations and produced databases that described their holdings. Libraries eventually developed online catalogs that used a computer display terminal to allow users to search and display records, providing much more convenient and powerful ways to locate library materials.

Online catalogs evolved through many generations, in tandem with changes happening in the larger realm of computing hardware and software. Mainframe terminals gave way to personal computers and graphical interfaces. As the Web emerged, libraries quickly took to this medium. Web-based online catalogs allowed libraries to provide the means for users to search their collections from home or in the library using the same interface.

Libraries embraced the Web from its earliest years. Web-based library catalogs were among the first information resources on the Web. In 1995, when I edited the *Mecklermedia's Official Internet World World Wide Web Yellow Pages* (IDG Books, 1996), libraries represented a major portion of the then-finite number of sites available at that time. Web-based online catalogs emerged in 1995, with a Web gateway from VTLS and Sirsi Corporation's WebCat being some of the earliest examples. These early Web-based catalogs offered quite simple interfaces that allowed users to enter search terms and view results, including the location and status of any given item. Over time Web-based online catalogs gained an increasing number of features, including more sophisticated searching capabilities, new display options, as well as personalized self-service features.

The Web that we experience today has changed enormously from those earlier times. The broader Web has undergone very rapid and far-reaching changes. In the earliest days, the Web was dominated by academic interests. But this phase was short-lived as commercial interests entered the scene. E-commerce transformed the Web into a medium for the general public, driving the need to offer services through interfaces that could be easily understood. Interest in the Web exploded and sparked incredible development. The initial pace of growth could not be sustained, leading to what is called the burst of the dot.com bubble in 2001. Even after this period, interest in the Web continued, with steadily increasing numbers of persons using the Web.

The Web passed a threshold of fundamental change in about 2004 that many saw as the beginning of a new era, dubbed Web 2.0. O'Reilly Media first used this term to characterize the transformations in Web technologies toward more social interactions, multimedia content, and dynamic presentation. Social networks on the Web have become a major phenomenon, with large portions of the general public engaged with sites such as Facebook, MySpace, Flickr, Twitter, and LinkedIn. Although the history of the Web spans only a brief moment in history, the changes in the technologies that comprise the medium and its impact on society are enormous.

▶ THE STATUS QUO: LEGACY ONLINE CATALOGS

Unfortunately, the products that libraries relied on for their online catalogs evolved at a slower pace than the rapid advancements both in the Web and in the way that library collections have evolved toward ever-increasing portions of electronic content. The two major problems with the earlier generation of Web-based online catalogs include a narrow scope that fails to address the full breadth of library collections and user interfaces that lag behind the conventions used on Web destinations outside the library.

Narrow Scope

In the current phase of library automation, most libraries offer a Web-based online catalog, usually delivered as a module of an ILS. These online catalogs provide access to the material managed within the ILS, which includes books, periodicals, and other materials.

Library collections span at least three major categories of content, managed and accessed through different platforms. The ILS manages the inventory of materials that libraries purchase. Licensed content, e-journal collections, databases of aggregated content, and other resources rely on tools such as OpenURL link resolvers, federated search, and electronic resource management systems. Libraries deal with local special collections with yet another set of tools. Local digital collections of photographs, manuscripts, and the like will be managed through digital asset management systems such as CONTENTdm. Physical collections may be managed through a separate system of finding aids, usually based on EAD (Encoded Archival Description) software.

It's common practice for libraries to position the online catalog module of their ILS as the primary search interface on their Web site. But as library collections increasingly include content not directly represented in the ILS, the online catalog can no longer serve as a comprehensive search tool.

One of the main problems with the traditional online catalog is that it does not include sufficient information regarding the deeper contents of a collection. Library users simply aren't familiar with the ways that libraries organize and provide access to their collections. We in libraries understand that the ILS manages collections at a fairly high level. We catalog the titles of the books, but not the individual chapters. We describe the periodicals and journals titles, and manage the span of coverage and issues received, but we don't describe the individual articles. Within the ILS we may provide a record for a special image collection that the library has created, but it is not common to include descriptions of individual images.

Library users don't necessarily understand that the online catalog, positioned as the main search interface on a library's Web site, isn't the place to search for articles, book chapters, or the contents of a library's digital collections. They don't realize that the interface doesn't search the full texts of the materials—as they are used to elsewhere on the Web.

One of the major limitations of the current generation of online catalogs involves its superficial coverage of the library's periodical collection. While the ILS may describe all of the periodical titles held by the library, it does not address all of the articles held within them. The description of periodicals at the article level has historically happened outside the ILS. A library's periodical collection contains a vast number of articles. Libraries rely on abstracting and indexing products that specialize in describing the individual articles held within the periodical literature.

Libraries struggle with the problem of finding the best way to provide access to their growing collections of electronic content. It's common for libraries to offer multiple approaches. They may offer an alphabetical list of the e-journals and databases, a searchable database of e-journal titles or other finding aids, or a metasearch tool to simplify end-user searching of these resources.

To search for individual articles, libraries often direct users to products to which they subscribe that offer searchable indexes within specified areas of interest, some broad, and some highly specialized. A typical library Web site will include links to these information products so that users can search for articles according to topic, keywords, and subjects.

As these lists of resources have grown to unwieldy proportions, products have emerged to streamline the approach for library users. Often termed "metasearches" or "federated searches," these tools allow a user to enter a search and find results from many different resources. In a metasearch, an interface prompts the user to enter search terms, which are then transmitted to several preselected information resources. The results from each of the target resources are then collected and presented to the user. The information sent and received between the metasearch product and the target resources takes place behind the scenes, saving the user from having to guess which targets might be appropriate to select or deal with the different interfaces of each target resource.

Metasearch, while a convenient tool, has some inherent limitations, mostly involving the speed with which they return results, the depth of the results, and the difficulty of sorting results by relevancy. Metasearch happens in real time, making these tools vulnerable to the vagaries of Internet bandwidth and to the performance of any given target. They must also make compromises in processing results. Even if a search matches thousands of items in a target resource, only the first few records are transmitted in the initial result list. Despite these limitations, metasearch tools allow a simplified approach for finding journal articles. Metasearch products do not solve the entire problem. We'll see later that metasearch technology often forms a component of discovery interfaces.

The status quo for many libraries involves a disjointed approach to providing access to their collections and services through their Web sites. When it comes to finding content within the library's diverse collections, there are too many starting points. A user has to know to start with the online catalog when looking for print materials, look in an e-journal database when looking for articles, and check the institutional repository or other digital repositories when looking for locally produced content. Framed this way, the problem is broader than the online catalog. Wouldn't it be great to offer a search environment that spans all these different aspects of library content?

Interface Issues

The other part of the problem with the older online catalogs involves the interfaces they employ. While one must be careful not to paint all the online catalog products with the same brush, some general observations apply. The older style online catalogs tend toward complexity, rely heavily on text, and haven't adopted many of the user interface conventions broadly used elsewhere on the Web.

The conventional online catalog interface may give an option between a simple and an advanced search. The advanced search allows the user to provide a number of qualifiers to be entered to narrow the result set. The proper use of these qualifiers may not be readily apparent to library users, and may require some knowledge of Boolean operators. To deal with the complexity of library catalogs, many libraries offer instruction sessions to explain the intricacies of the interface, what's included or not included, and how to use it effectively. Library users don't find most of the old-style library catalogs self-explanatory.

The traditional online catalog looks more like interfaces typical of the earlier generation of the Web rather than what users experience on modern-day Web sites. Some traditional characteristics include the following:

- ▶ The interfaces are mostly text based. This contrasts with more modern sites that incorporate images, video, and other multimedia.
- ▶ They lack the visual aspects that are now standard throughout the Web. The look of most professionally built Web sites can be stunning, with creative use of design, graphics, style, and color that is visually appealing and intuitively functional. Web-based catalogs haven't lived up to this level of presentation, offering a plain, somewhat primitive, appearance.
- ▶ They deliver results in ordered lists, usually alphabetical by author or title.
- ▶ They depend on terminology specific to the library that may not be well-understood by the general public.
- ▶ They do not compensate for misspelled words or offer suggestions for alternative or related terms.

Next-Generation Concepts

For a period, libraries seemed a little complacent regarding their Web-based online catalogs relative to the broader realm of the Web. But we're now in a phase where libraries recognize the vital importance of providing their content and services in ways more in tune with what our users experience beyond the library.

Our users come to library Web sites with expectations set by their broader experience of the Web. These expectations apply both to the look and feel of the interface and to the delivery of content.

A new generation of discovery layer interfaces is emerging that provides the means for libraries to meet these expectations. Engaging users on the Web through current technologies forms part of a strategy to increase library relevancy. Libraries ignore modernizing their Web sites at their own peril.

The Competition

In today's society, at least in the developed world, most library users have become quite accustomed to the Web. They routinely visit many other destinations that provide an endless variety of services, information, and recreation.

Many of the popular Web destinations overlap with services offered by libraries. Libraries do not hold a monopoly on organizing and providing access to information on the Web. Search engines, publishers, booksellers, and other content providers have commercial interests in delivering information to the public, compensated through direct sales or revenue associated with advertising. Libraries aim to provide high-quality information without cost to these same individuals, yet struggle to gain their attention.

Today's Web users routinely experience search capabilities of enormous power. Many expect to type in a couple of words about a given topic and instantly receive a few highly relevant results culled from billions of Web pages. The incredible sophistication of search engines such as Google have acclimated users to expect almost magical results.

E-commerce is now a common Web activity. A large portion of the population regularly makes purchases through the Web. Sites that specialize in online sales depend on exceptional search capabilities and simple ease of use for their financial success. Their customers must be able to find and select items for purchase out of a vast inventory database. The user interfaces on these commercial Web sites must be self-explanatory. If a customer cannot easily navigate through the Web site and make use of its services, the business will suffer. Such sites follow design principles that guide their users through a flow that yields desired results—usually terminating with a purchase.

Given the elegant and powerful sites that permeate the Web, libraries need to work hard to deliver their services in a way that will impress their users. Leaving legacy products in place can erode the library's standing, at least to some segments of its user population. It's quite a challenge to provide a new approach for the growing ranks of Web-savvy users while preserving something familiar to other library users who rely on the traditional online catalog.

Next-Generation Systems to Meet Current Needs

We've pointed out some of the shortcomings of the current line of library catalogs. Fortunately, there's relief in sight. The development of a new generation of products is well underway. Almost all of the companies involved in developing library automation software have some kind of new offering in addition to those created directly by libraries. We'll talk about the particulars in Chapter 3, but the products in this arena form one of the most rapidly growing areas in the industry.

Some automation companies are enhancing the online catalog component of their ILS with next-gen features. Others offer separate products that can be used with their own or their competitors' ILS. Separating the interface from the core automation system is now a common approach. We see a few companies not involved in creating core library automation systems that have jumped into the market. Content companies have also joined the fray, expanding the scope of their products.

Interesting work is also taking place with open source products. Libraries and other organizations have created alternatives that compete closely with those produced by the commercial companies. Open source software development now represents another major movement in library automation. The emergence of fully functional open source products, which don't have the license fees associated with proprietary products, stirs up the dynamics. Open source alternatives put pressure on those developing proprietary products to add value and moderate the cost, and they have become established, compelling products in their own right.

No Universal Path

I recognize that not all libraries have the same needs and expectations. It would be presumptuous to assert that every library needs to ditch its current library catalog and replace it with a newer alternative. Some libraries may have a well-defined set of needs that are well served with a traditional online catalog, especially those involved with primarily print collections.

A few of the library catalogs delivered with ILS products aren't so traditional. One very reasonable path that several companies involved in developing library automation systems have followed takes the course of enhancing their online catalog modules to embrace many of the characteristics of the next generation. This path may provide a smoother path forward than the alternative of implementing something completely new.

I encourage readers to critically consider the current set of products and components that comprise their public interface and determine where they fit on the continuum spanning from obsolete to next generation. Some libraries may find the need for a minor tune-up. Others may realize they need a complete overhaul, and some may have already made the transition to one of these new products.

Urgency for Change

More than any other technology product, the interfaces that libraries provide their users involve the highest stakes. While it's also important for libraries to use automation software that helps them manage their internal operations as efficiently as possible, the products they use to interact directly with users have a much more immediate impact. As libraries deploy better tools for delivering access to their collections, they will become more relevant destinations for their users and may even become strong competitors to the commercial alternatives.

Libraries need a new generation of interfaces that will help leverage their investments in electronic content. As libraries invest increasing amounts of their resources in subscriptions to electronic resources and other digital content, it's important to also invest in tools that will help users find the new content. Libraries that continue to rely on only a traditional online catalog may lack the best tools available to provide access to all aspects of their collections.

We've seen how quickly time moves in the development of new cycles of technology and in the evolution of the Web. Yet, new products take several years to become established in libraries because libraries have a tendency to wait and see how any given trend will play out before making a move. In the realm of Web-based technologies that evolve at a rapid pace this strategy has led to libraries holding on to products for too long that don't compare well with what users see elsewhere on the Web.

Furthermore, libraries unfortunately do not always have adequate funds at their disposal to rapidly deploy new technologies. Planning cycles tend to be long, and many projects compete for funding. There seems to be a built-in tension between rapidly changing Web technologies and slower-moving library planning cycles.

The implementation of a discovery interface will give libraries added flexibility as they manage changes in the automation environment. Most of the discovery interfaces will operate with many different ILS products. A library might choose to implement a new discovery interface with its legacy ILS in order to make a more immediate improvement for its end users with less cost and in a shorter timeframe than a wholesale replacement of its automation infrastructure. At a later date the library could then replace its legacy ILS with little or no perceptible changes for its patrons. Many libraries are following this strategy of implementing a new discovery interface in the short term and deferring the replacement of the full legacy ILS.

Next-generation discovery interfaces, while still evolving, include some relatively mature products. In terms of Web timeframes, the concept of next-generation library interfaces isn't especially recent, with products such as AquaBrowser coming on the scene as early as 2002. It was about 2006 when this software genre became especially competitive with the launch of products such as Primo and Encore. An open source option, VuFind, became available in about 2007. Yet, new products continue to emerge. One recent trend involves discovery services that come populated with indexes that provide access to large quantities of content. Serials Solutions, EBSCO, OCLC, and Ex Libris each made announcements in 2009 that they would combine new-generation interface technologies with large bodies of indexed content.

The age of new library interfaces has arrived. We can expect the majority of libraries to adopt one of these new discovery interfaces over the next few years. The remaining chapters of this book aim to provide practical information to help guide you through the process of understanding this new genre of software, selecting the one best suited to your library's needs, and managing its implementation, assess its impact, and look forward to yet more change in the future.

▶2

PLANNING

▶ Craft a Great User Interface

▶ Address the Full Range of Library Collections

▶ Understand the Product Options

▶ Lay the Groundwork

▶ Select and Procure a Discovery Interface

▶ Follow a Process Based on User-Centered Design

We've established that the traditional online catalog cannot properly function as the primary tool for providing access to library content and services. Libraries today need a fresh approach, one designed for the complex collections they offer and for users ever more tech savvy on the Web. In this chapter, I describe some of the basic concepts, features, and technologies embodied by the products that fall within this new genre of discovery layer products.

▶ CRAFT A GREAT USER INTERFACE

As we move into the next generation of discovery interfaces for libraries, one of the lessons learned from the backlash against the previous generation involves a new focus on ease of use. If the mechanics of using the interface frustrate the user, it will not live up to its full potential in providing access to the great content that a library offers.

I often hear online catalogs being characterized as unwieldy and difficult to figure out. Yet, once mastered, they excel at delivering predictable and systematic results. The challenge for today involves honing systems that are easy to use yet still function as sophisticated tools for information retrieval.

A great interface should be self-explanatory and avoid the use of techniques that require instruction. Keep in mind that the vast majority of the use of these systems will take place outside the physical confines of the library. If your patrons can't figure out how to use the features of the interface on their own, then it's not met the ideal level of usability. No site out on the commercial Web would prosper if its user interface wasn't self-explanatory.

For as long as I have been involved with computers, one of the main goals has been to create intuitive interfaces. Although no one is born knowing how to operate a computer, it's helpful to employ controls that operate like other devices that a person encounters in everyday life. As computers become more pervasive, we can choose from a palate of techniques that have proven successful.

One of the most important factors today for library interfaces involves consistency with interface techniques employed elsewhere on the Web. An increasing proportion of library users are well acclimated to the way that Web interfaces work on mainstream destinations. The way that links, mouseovers, menus, search boxes, results lists, and many other components that comprise an interface have become imprinted on users as they experience the Web. If libraries deviate too far from the established norms of the Web, we place our patrons in unfamiliar territory.

Commercial Web sites do everything possible to make things easy for the user. High monetary stakes in terms of product sold or advertising revenue provide enormous motivation to hone interfaces to perfection. Those who develop library interfaces do well to pay close attention to what's going on in the search, e-commerce, and social networking spaces and learn from these interfaces used by millions.

The new generation of library interfaces aims to embrace a high standard for usability. In today's environment it's just expected that Web-based services allow users to think about what they want to accomplish on the site, not about the mechanics of operating the interface.

The site should have a natural flow that leads users to the desired goal. For library interfaces, this generally means guiding the user through expressing a search, viewing results, making selections, and viewing content.

A successful library interface can take a variety of forms. When we look at commercial sites, we observe that the popular ones run a wide spectrum from clean and simple such as the classic Google search page to Amazon.com with a rich set of features and options. Likewise, we'll see some library discovery layer products that take the clean-and-simple approach of the bare search box while others present a richer set of controls to the user on the initial entry page.

Practical Tip

Spend some time exploring nonlibrary Web sites, paying close attention to the look and feel of the interface and to the conventions used for search, navigation, and presentation. Make mental notes on whether users familiar with these sites would find your library's current online catalog or the specific replacement products under consideration to be familiar and comfortable.

We've established the importance of crafting a great interface. Next, let's consider some of the major features and characteristics of the new discovery layer products that contribute toward a friendlier, more self-explanatory interface for library users.

Optimized for Library Users

It's important to recognize the audience of the new discovery interfaces. They target library users and therefore may not be entirely satisfactory for all the needs of library personnel. The native interfaces of the integrated library system (ILS), institutional repositories, and the other systems that populate the discovery interface will not go away, enabling library personnel to take advantage of their more deterministic features. A recent OCLC study, "Online Catalogs: What Users and Librarians Want" (Calhoun et al., 2009), based on survey data, documents major differences in the expectations that end users bring to the interface as pertains to the needs of librarians and library staff: Librarians' perspectives about data quality remain highly influenced by classic principles of information organization, while end users' expectations of data quality arise from their experiences of how information is organized on popular Web sites. Maintaining a clear perspective that these discovery interfaces target end users may alleviate some of the temptation to clutter the features or to compromise their performance to accommodate features needed by library personnel.

Relevancy Ranked Results

An important feature that the new discovery products borrow from the broader Web search arena has to do with the ordering of results. Almost all search engines on the Web list results according to relevancy, with the items most strongly related to the query terms appearing first.

Traditional online library catalogs present lists of results in a deterministic order, such as alphabetically or chronologically so that the most recent material appears first. This method of ordering results lists, while systematic, does not give users much help in identifying the materials most relevant to their query. The ability to order lists either alphabetically or chronologically will continue to be an essential feature for those who need to view comprehensive results, although most next-generation interfaces offer relevance ordering as the default sort option.

While the general idea of ordering results according to relevancy seems simple on the surface, it requires a great deal of sophisticated computing behind the scenes. Many factors come into play when calculating relevancy. The way that the words in the record match the search terms can identify the list of candidates for the results set. If the query involves multiple words, records that contain more of the terms will count as more relevant. Those that contain the exact phrase might appear highest on the list.

The nuances involved in determining relevancy seem almost endless. A relevancy-based search environment has to exploit many different factors to provide satisfactory results. Should matches in one field count as more relevant than in other fields? We would expect that a match in the title of an entry to count as more relevant, for example, than if it appears in a note field.

Search engines can also use social data to help determine relevancy. Apart from the empirical word matching, data on how frequently users select a given item in response to a term adds a strong measure of relevancy. In a group of items equally ranked by empirical measures, data indicating that users almost always pick a given item gives strong evidence of higher relevancy. While relevancy shouldn't necessarily take the form of a popularity contest, social use data provides a valuable added dimension to determining relevancy.

The issues of determining relevancy for results involving library content invokes a number of challenges that may not arise in general search or e-commerce environments. If a user types in a name, are works written by the person more relevant than works about the person? If the work is available in multiple formats, which should be listed first? Should relevancy favor the popularity of material or scholarly content?

It's especially difficult to perform relevancy ranking when addressing mixed collections. If, for example, the body of content includes books, represented by MARC records, and a collection of full-text articles, it's difficult to calculate proper relevancy when the metadata strategies differ so widely. The key challenge involves finding ways to balance the calculation of relevancy to ensure reasonable representation of items among all the different collection components.

Preferences for the various weightings of factors used to score relevancy will vary. In most cases, there will be some documentation about how the product determines relevancy, and there may be options for a library to fine-tune this feature. Search engines that sort by relevance use some kind of mathematical scoring system.

Users expect results to be returned in a relevancy ranked order. Calculating the best way to determine relevancy in a library interface presents enormous challenges. In a generalized interface, it's difficult to predict the kind of material that the user will find most interesting or important. If the user types in the name of an author, should the resources written by the author be ranked ahead of biographies or critical works? In response to a term such as "harry potter," should it return the most recent book in this popular series? In many relevancy-based library interfaces I often find that books on themes found in the series rank ahead of the works themselves. In a public library, it seems that most users would be interested in the latest available book in the series. In an academic library, primary sources and materials based on peer-reviewed scholarly research should list ahead of informal secondary sources.

Practical Tip

When considering discovery layer products, put their relevancy engines through their paces. Look for implementations that most closely match the profile of your own library, according to type (academic, public, medical, legal, etc.) and collection size.

Faceted Navigation

One of the key problems with search environments involves helping users find the items they want out of a large set of results. Sorting results by relevancy helps, but a good interface needs additional methods. One popular technique uses facets to limit the presentation of results.

Faceted navigation allows users to incrementally narrow the search results. Through the presentation of relevant facets, the interface guides the user from a list of results too large to scan, to progressively smaller sets until the user arrives at a short list of items within a specific area of interest (see Figure 2.1).

▶ Figure 2.1: Faceted Navigation

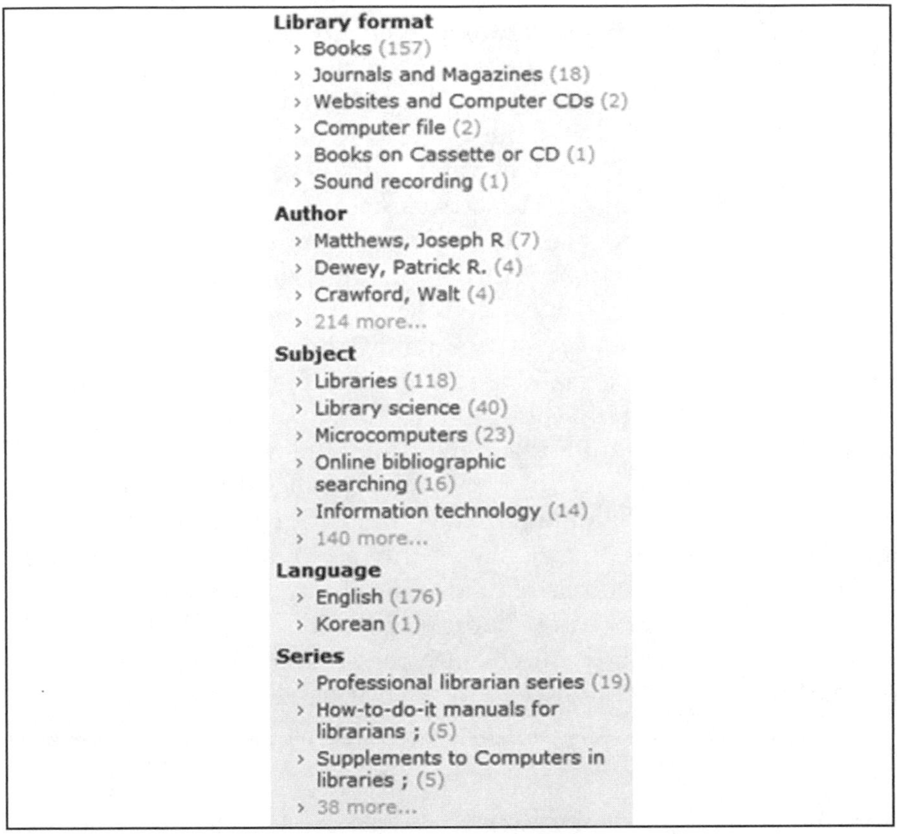

Library format
> Books (157)
> Journals and Magazines (18)
> Websites and Computer CDs (2)
> Computer file (2)
> Books on Cassette or CD (1)
> Sound recording (1)

Author
> Matthews, Joseph R (7)
> Dewey, Patrick R. (4)
> Crawford, Walt (4)
> 214 more...

Subject
> Libraries (118)
> Library science (40)
> Microcomputers (23)
> Online bibliographic searching (16)
> Information technology (14)
> 140 more...

Language
> English (176)
> Korean (1)

Series
> Professional librarian series (19)
> How-to-do-it manuals for librarians ; (5)
> Supplements to Computers in libraries ; (5)
> 38 more...

In most cases the facets will be presented in groups, with individual clickable terms under each heading. Facets help users navigate from broad general results to a smaller, more manageable, set of specific results. This interface technique provides a convenient way for users to drill down through the collection without having a great deal of knowledge in advance of the kinds of materials that might be available.

An interface that uses faceted navigation will display the facets that the user has selected, as a reminder of the context of the current search results. It's also expected that there be some way to easily de-select a facet and update the search results presented accordingly. This feature makes it much easier for users to explore the collection by trying out the various facets.

Most interfaces that use faceted navigation display the number of items that will be returned from the current result set when it is selected. This number provides helpful information to the user regarding the importance of the term. Limited space is available to present a long list of facet terms that appear under each category heading. The initial display of the results may present a few of the facets with highest result counts, with a link that allows users to view more if interested in exploring further. It's not practical to display a comprehensive list of all the facets available under each category. Rather, it's common to offer a sampling of the top terms that can be easily expanded as needed.

Most sites that use this feature use narrow columns to represent facets expressed in the collection. The most important categories of facets are presented first, because the columns can be long and run below the part of the page that displays without scrolling.

In a library environment, facets can be presented for a wide variety of categories, including these common groups:

- ▶ Formats (e.g., book, journal, article, images, video, scores, sound recordings)
- ▶ Authors (personal, corporate)
- ▶ Topics (subject headings, terms based on LC classification numbers, geographical setting)
- ▶ Locations (physical branch location, department, special collection)
- ▶ Language
- ▶ Date of publication (often given as a range)

Some interfaces also use facets to limit results to online content, a handy feature for distance learners for whom visiting the library in person may not be convenient. Similarly, some products present facets based on circulation status, making it easy to browse through only those items not currently checked out.

The facets presented usually derive from specific fields in the metadata that describe the collection. High-quality consistent metadata produces more effective faceted navigation.

Visually Enriched Displays

To grab the attention of users, it's important for a next-gen discovery interface to have great visual appeal. The expectations for the looks of a site have risen dramatically since the days of legacy catalogs. Today, even if a site functions well but has a drab appearance, it may not make a great impression on your users.

It's also important to keep in mind that some users rely on visual information more than others. For some users, an image catches their attention much more than purely textual information.

It's become increasingly expected for library interfaces to offer some kind of visual representation of the items returned in search results. Library catalogs now routinely incorporate images associated with book jackets, DVDs, CDs, and the like. This feature isn't limited to next-gen products—many of the standard catalogs support this feature.

A main issue with this feature involves finding a source for the images. It's not necessarily practical for a library to create images on its own by scanning its materials. Rather, libraries can obtain images through paid subscription services or through free sources.

In most cases the images are not stored on the library's servers but are displayed on demand from the provider's site. As an item displays in the library's catalog, it sends a query to the image provider's server behind the scenes and automatically embeds a link to the image within the page if it is available.

The services that offer images also offer textual materials that enhance the display, such as summaries, reviews, and tables of contents. Standard library catalog records may not include these elements, which can contain information of great benefit to the user. When this information is layered in at the point of display, it does not contribute to the discovery process. To assist in the search process, these textual enrichment components would need to be harvested and indexed in advance.

Commercial services for visual and textual enrichment elements include Syndetic Solutions, which is part of R.R. Bowker (www.bowker .com/syndetics), and Content Café 2 from Baker & Taylor (www.btol .com/pdfs/content_cafe.pdf). These companies have an annual subscription fee, scaled to the library's size. Many libraries take advantage of free services such as the Amazon Product Advertising API (http:// aws.amazon.com) and the Google Book Search APIs (http://code .google.com/apis/books). Before using one of the free services, it's prudent to carefully read their terms of service. Amazon Product Advertising API License Agreement, for example, currently requires display of links back to its site (https://affiliate-program.amazon.com/ gp/advertising/api/detail/agreement.html; see especially Section 2).

Search Term Recommendations

"No items found" is the least helpful response that a system can give to a user. It's important to give users as much help as possible to get them started with their search rather than issuing an abrupt message. A number of techniques can help the user find something in the library's collection in response to even an improperly formulated search. Spelling errors, typos, or simply lack of knowledge of library cataloging conventions should not be insurmountable barriers to finding results. A good search environment will work proactively to deliver meaningful results, presenting recommendations for queries that may provide more effective results than the characters typed into the search box.

Recommendation features have been standard parts of Web search engines for many years. Google's "Did you mean" feature has made an enormous impact. It's become commonplace to turn to Google when we don't know how to spell a word or a name, knowing that it will almost certainly understand what we meant and give the proper term.

Such recommendations go well beyond spelling corrections. Just correcting the spelling of a term does not help that much if the corrected term also yields no results. A good recommendation system will use spelling correction, phonetic indexing, related terms from authority records, and many other techniques to help guide the user into formulating a query that matches their intent. The service may check several variations of plausible search terms against the search engine to know which one returns the most results before it presents a recommendation. This technique shouldn't be applied only when the query supplied by the user yields zero hits. If a given term returns a very small number of items and a slight variation will return many more, then it might notify the user.

Many search environments have taken this service further by helping the user find a search term even before striking the Enter key. These features, often called "autocomplete" or "type-ahead," take the letters that a user has typed and begin to query the search engine for possible terms that appear below the search box. If one of these happens to be what the user intends, it can be selected with a keystroke or two rather than having to type the rest of the query. This feature not only saves some typing but also provides very helpful information on the content available and on the proper form of the terms.

"More Like This": Recommended Related Resources

On the commercial Web, it is now common for some searches to not only respond with direct search results but also to make recommendations of items that do not necessarily match the user's query but have some kind of direct or indirect relationship implied by the context. E-commerce sites have financial motivation to place additional products in front of their customers. They can exploit their sales data to reveal relationships among products: "Customers who purchased item A also purchased item B."

Libraries have an interest in making suggestions of additional items to their patrons. These recommendations could be based on other recent works by the same author, frequently circulated items within the same classification scheme, or other triggers that provide some indication that the user might find the item worthwhile.

Personalization

A Web site can offer additional features to users willing to register and sign in. Services offered by traditional library catalogs include the ability to view the materials currently checked out, issue renewal requests, place requests to be notified when items become available, make interlibrary loan requests, pay fines, and many other actions that might otherwise require a visit to the library. Self-service through the Web site has become increasingly expected.

Personalization also enables the use of customized settings related to search and retrieval. Users might want to save search results for future consultation, bookmark specific items, or establish preferences regarding narrowing searches to their favorite databases or disciplines. Notification services also tie in to personalization, such as the ability to set up alerts to be notified by e-mail when the library obtains new materials in a specific area of interest.

User-Contributed Reviews and Rankings

One of the seminal characteristics of the Web today is its high level of engagement with users. Flat, one-way presentation of information has given way to active involvement by users who increasingly want to be contributors of content, not merely its consumers. Today the typical Web user might upload videos to YouTube, post to a blog, comment on others' blogs, write book reviews on Amazon, upload photos to Flickr or Facebook, or post details of their thoughts and actions on Twitter.

While library interfaces primarily exist to deliver information, they can also provide opportunities for users to contribute and interact. Some of the social features in next-gen catalogs include the ability for users to add tags to items, provide rankings, and write comments or reviews. This user-contributed content can supplement the official metadata supplied by the library in terms of both access points for search and guidance on the quality of the material.

Two issues arise related to user contributions in library interfaces. Some libraries worry that information supplied by uses is not always appropriate for others. These libraries might prefer to screen content supplied by users before it displays it publicly. Another issue involves achieving a sufficient level of user engagement for the features to have a positive impact. The proportion of users to content items may be too low to result in a sufficient number of ratings, reviews, or tags to add value to the collection.

To reach a critical mass of user-contributed content, some libraries subscribe to services such as LibraryThing for Libraries (www.librarything .com/forlibraries), which draws from a massive database of user-generated reviews and tags so that user-contributed content appears on a large portion of the materials presented through the library catalog. ChiliFresh (www.chilifresh.com) offers a similar product that integrates with library catalogs for the submission and display of user-contributed reviews, sharing the reviews among all participating libraries.

Record Groups of Related Materials

When presenting lists of results, many of the discovery products simplify the display with record grouping techniques. Record grouping consistent with the Functional Requirements for Bibliographic Records (FRBR) model has been widely discussed in libraries for a number of years, but it has not been possible to implement in most of the legacy interfaces. Following the principles of FRBR, related items are collapsed under a single entry until selected. For any given work, FRBR recognizes multiple levels of related material, following a hierarchy of manifestations, expressions, and items.

FRBR provides a structure for the way that records can be grouped together as presented through an interface. It presents the basic work as a single entry on a results list, allowing the user to display and select specific editions and formats and find a specific item. When considering a discovery interface, some libraries may find record groupings according to FRBR a valuable feature, although the details about how to systematically organize the records can be complex.

Tag Clouds

A feature common among Web 2.0 applications involves presenting terms that occur in a resource, often with fonts scaled larger proportionately to the relative importance of each term. These are called "tag clouds" and provide a visual conceptual map of the item. Users can click on any of the terms in the tag cloud to retrieve other related items.

Deep Indexing

As search environments evolve, it's increasingly expected, and possible, to base retrieval not just on metadata that describe a resource but also on the full content of the resource itself. Traditional library catalogs, for example, search based on the metadata in the field of MARC records. When searching collections of articles from e-journals, some products search against citations, but some index the full text of the articles. Internet search engines also index all the words in the pages, PDF files, and other content linked on the Web. Full-text searching offers extremely powerful retrieval capability, where every word or phrase anywhere in the material becomes a possible point of access. Metadata-based searching works efficiently, especially when based on high-quality cataloging.

It wasn't that long ago when the idea of digitizing all the books in the world seemed completely unrealistic. But today, with the advent of the Google Library Book project, the Open Content Alliance, and other mass digitization initiatives, we can anticipate a time when electronic versions of almost all books will be available. While copyright laws may restrict how digitized books can be presented for reading, the real power of these electronic texts comes into play in the discovery arena. The ability to create indexes and search against the full text of books will enable an incredibly powerful search environment.

Most of the discovery interfaces operate on the basis of harvesting content from multiple target repositories, processing them into a centralized index, and making a wide variety of materials available through a single search. Increasingly, these centralized indexes include not only metadata in the form of citations for articles or MARC records for books but also the full text of the material. Creating a search environment that represents a large universe of content, spanning many different formats and based on a composite of metadata and full text, is complex but pays off in sophisticated search capabilities.

Even when the full text of a resource can be indexed into the search environment, it's important to include any other metadata available as well. While the full text provides a great deal of raw data for the search engine, high-quality metadata are essential for creating facets, determining relevancy, and supporting structured queries. Next-gen library interfaces need to adopt more full-text search capabilities to be on par with what users experience through commercial sites.

Virtual Shelf Browsing

Next-gen library catalogs aim to provide a variety of tools to enhance the users' ability to find material within the library's collection. To the largest extent possible, it's desirable to offer as rich of an experience to those who visit the Web site as to those who frequent its physical premises. Within the walls of the library, patrons may use the online catalog to find specific materials, but they're just as likely to browse the shelves, hoping to find something of interest. Libraries work hard to assign meaningful call numbers to materials to facilitate this way of exploring the library—peruse the shelves, pick up an item that catches your eye, read a few pages, repeat until satisfied.

Several discovery interfaces re-create this part of the in-library experience. By taking advantage of the call numbers and shelving location, it's possible to build an interface that reproduces shelf arrangement, allowing convenient navigation to browse to the left and right of the position of the current item. Combining the navigation by call number with images of cover art and full-text snippets can closely approximate the experience of browsing inside the library.

It's also common for libraries to select and feature books in the library through special displays, much like we're used to seeing in bookstores. This experience can also easily be conveyed in the library catalog by displaying a set of images that represent featured items on the library Web site and other relevant contexts in the catalog. Any time that a user clicks on an image, full information for the item displays; supplying a snippet of text, a video clip, or other relevant content helps mimic the in-library experience.

Visual Search Tools

Library search interfaces tend to be text oriented. Even the new search techniques embraced by the new generation of library catalogs primarily operate on the basis of queries supplied in words. Many users, however, approach problems visually and find purely text-based queries less intuitive. A variety of search tools have been devised that allow users to formulate queries or view results visually. Groxis, for example, developed a graphical visual search interface that was adopted by libraries such as Stanford University. This company met its demise in early 2009. Other tools that follow more visual techniques include the "cloud of associations" presented in the AquaBrowser interface and tag clouds such as that used in Innovative Interfaces' Encore product.

Connections with External Applications

Library catalogs aren't part of the daily lives of library users, so information and services need to be offered through other means in addition to the traditional Web site or catalog. Discovery layer platforms need to be integrated into other information applications both within the library and its parent organization and externally. The specific applications will vary and include course management systems or other learning environments and identity management systems.

Desired features of a **course management system** include the abilities to plant a search box on a course page preconfigured to query resources relevant to the topic and to present reading materials from the library's collection of electronic content selected by the instructor or librarian subject specialist. Discovery layer products often need to tie into the authentication environments of the broader organization, so they also need an **identity management system**. A person should be able to sign on once and then take advantage of network services offered by all parts of the organization. A student, for example, should be able to enter a username and password once and have access to e-mail, the course management system, financial accounts, and library services.

The ability to integrate these types of features depends on how well the discovery product supports Web services and other application programming interfaces (APIs). A robust and well-documented API will allow the library great flexibility in connecting with its users through a variety of systems, including others within the library's own environment and in external applications.

▶ ADDRESS THE FULL RANGE OF LIBRARY COLLECTIONS

Next-gen discovery interfaces aim to provide comprehensive access to the broad range of resources that comprise a library's collection, such as the ILS, the body of articles included in subscriptions to e-journals and aggregated databases, as well as repositories of local content in many forms. The ideal next-gen interface will provide a single point of entry to all of a library's content.

Although the interfaces function according to a variety of approaches, they do have some points in common. One is that, to address many different types of content, the interfaces rely on some type of search engine technology based on a consolidated index created by harvesting the metadata or full-text content from one or more external repositories. The general architecture of the discovery interfaces follows a model of comprehensive harvesting content from repositories and creating a centralized index.

The idea of searching multiple resources through a single interface has been around for a long time. Since the earliest days of online catalogs, the Z39.50 protocol has enabled search and retrieval among multiple bibliographic systems. A given Z39.50 client can address multiple targets to allow users to search many different resources and be presented with unified results. This protocol, and more modern XML-based alternatives, is the basis of metasearch products that deliver results in real time from many resources. While this model of federated search continues to have many pragmatic uses, it's not the favored approach today.

The modern approach to searching multiple stores of content involves harvesting and indexing. Rather than requesting records in response to queries in real time, this approach fetches all of the records of a resource in advance and feeds them into a search engine to create a comprehensive index. Harvesting the entire repository may sound like an unwieldy process, but it really isn't a problem with today's large-scale hardware and generous bandwidth. Harvesting shifts the consumption of resources to the early stage of harvesting and indexing processes that take place prior to end-user searching. This method results in fast search performance because it works against a pre-built index. Index-based searching presents lists of results. The actual display of an item may involve interaction with the original repository. In the case of the bibliographic information from the ILS, the discovery interface may display a full record based on harvested MARC records.

One of the hallmarks of next-gen discovery interfaces involves the use of pre-harvested content in a centralized index spanning the broadest representation possible of the library's collections. The search engine indexes the content in advance, performing all the processing necessary to ensure rapid search, relevancy ranking, and presentation of facets when the query is posed.

The initial wave of discovery layer products provides the environment in which a library can harvest and index any metadata or content to which it has access. Under normal circumstances, these data sources include the MARC records extracted from the ILS as well as metadata associated with institutional repositories, digital collections, and metadata or content from external open access resources.

E-journals and their content present the most difficult challenge for discovery interface products. We've noted that the native model of these products involves comprehensive harvesting of metadata or full texts in advance. This task can be much harder to accomplish with e-journal content, because all the articles involve an incredible amount of content and that content resides within the proprietary systems managed by commercial publishers.

Given the difficulty in harvesting e-journal content, many of the discovery products use federated search technology to include this content within search results. While techniques differ, it's common to address the preharvested content in a default search, with an option to extend the search to e-journal content, retrieved through an integrated federated search component. While a pragmatic solution, this model does not quite meet the ultimate vision of the discovery interface as addressing equally print and electronic content.

It is only very recently that some companies have begun to offer prepopulated indexes of e-journal collections and other resources. Though it may not be practical for each individual library to harvest all the metadata that describes all of the articles represented within their e-journal collections, it is more feasible that an organization or company might be able to make arrangements with the publishers of e-journals and other electronic resources to provide citation or even full-text data of their content products for the purpose of indexing. Such a prepopulated index can then be offered to libraries for use within a discovery interface as a powerful tool for searching this important aspect of their collections.

The reach of a discovery product with a prepopulated index will vary according to the amount and type of the material represented. Ideally, the index would include all the content corresponding to a library's subscriptions.

In the realm of discovery, we aim for the widest possible scope of content. On the Web, we're used to search environments that address a global, near-compressive range of information. In the library arena, Web-scale discovery would aim to provide access to the full breadth of content represented in library collections. Achieving Web-scale discovery of library-provided content through comprehensive, preharvested indexes is an exceedingly ambitious goal. Yet, to meet the expectations of library users and to add value beyond general search tools such as Google Scholar, it's important to reach toward the ideal of indexing the full body of vetted library information.

The Role of the Federated Search   WITHDRAWN

As noted, one of the distinguishing characteristics of the new discovery interfaces involves the use of consolidated indexes built in advance through comprehensive harvesting of target resources. Unfortunately, it isn't always possible to gain access to the content in all of the resources of interest in order to populate these indexes. Yet, it's important to represent these resources in some way. The federated search, while it has its weaknesses as the primary search platform, can be used to extend the content addressed in the discovery interface to those that can't be comprehensively harvested in advance. Many of the discovery interfaces offer an optional integrated federated search component. How this type of federated search component operates varies among products, but, in general, users search against the native consolidated index first, with the ability to invoke additional results through the federated search.

Federated search results can take much longer to retrieve than those from the native index. Because this model of search and retrieval depends on real-time interactions with the servers of the information providers, the response times can vary and the number of items returned for any given search may be limited. Merging results returned from multiple targets and presenting them with relevancy ranking does not always work well. Although the federated search approach may not be ideal as the primary discovery method, it continues to provide a pragmatic way to extend the reach of a discovery interface to resources that cannot be harvested in advance.

Further issues to consider with a discovery interface project involve what content can be harvested and placed into its native interface and what resources can be represented through federated search. Identify which federated search product is supported. You may already have a federated search product and may be interested in applying it toward the discovery interface project. In most cases, the discovery interface may support only a specific federated search component.

▶ UNDERSTAND THE PRODUCT OPTIONS

We've covered some of the features of the new generation of discovery interfaces, as well as some future possibilities. Now, we will peruse the menu of products currently available within this genre. A wide assortment of selections awaits libraries ready to take the plunge to modernize the search tools they offer to their patrons. We'll look at open source, proprietary, locally installed, and hosted options.

In recent years, the idea of next-gen library catalogs has captured the attention of all fronts of the library automation industry. Many of the major companies offering an ILS have launched a new discovery layer product, in most cases offered as an independent product that can be used with competing ILSs as well as with their own. These companies include Innovative Interfaces (Encore), Ex Libris (Primo), SirsiDynix (Enterprise), and The Library Corporation (LS2 PAC). R.R. Bowker and Serials Solutions, involved in technology and content products outside the ILS arena, have become major players with AquaBrowser and Summon. EBSCO, primarily a publisher of electronic content products, has recently announced a discovery product. OCLC, the global nonprofit cooperative, positions WorldCat Local as a next-gen discovery interface and has revealed its intentions to provide core automation services.

Outside the commercial arena, library-led open source projects have produced alternatives such as VuFind from Villanova University, Blacklight from University of Virginia, and SOPAC from the Darien Public Library in Connecticut. Another strategy involves enhancing the online catalog of the ILS to incorporate the characteristics of next-gen products to save the libraries from having to acquire and install a separate product. Polaris Library Systems follows this tack for its commercial Polaris ILS as do the open source Koha and Evergreen automation systems.

The age of the primacy of OPAC is ending. While many libraries continue to use legacy catalogs supplied with their ILSs, little interest remains in new sales of these modules. Although the turnover rates for library products are generally slow, over the next few years we can expect to see a transition to this new generation of discovery layer products or revamped online catalogs.

The term "next-generation" is not limited to products that will be delivered sometime in the distant future. A variety of products are available now, and additional offerings have been announced for the near future. Undoubtedly, other new products will emerge, but libraries ready to move away from their traditional catalog will find ample options now.

Space does not permit a full review of each product, but I intend to provide enough information on the major alternatives available at the time of writing to whet your appetite. You will want to perform your own detailed analysis of all the relevant opportunities available in your area and for your type of library.

Most of the products can be seen in live use in libraries. Although some of the products have been out for a few years, adoption levels remain fairly modest. You can, however, find examples of most of them in use. As I survey the products, I'll point out some of the libraries that use them.

Practical Tip

Take time to explore a variety of the discovery products firsthand. Pay special attention to the ones implemented by libraries similar to your own, but be sure to try out a sufficient number of products to gain a sense of the full range of options.

Public, academic, and special libraries may be drawn to different products. Some are rather specialized, while others are designed for use by many different types of libraries.

It's not really possible to predict what these products will cost. Companies rarely set a fixed price for their software products or even make public the formula they use to determine the cost for a given library, and this is true for the new discovery interfaces as well. In general, the prices will vary based on the options selected and on the size and complexity of the library.

Profiles of Major Discovery Products

This section provides basic information about the major discovery interfaces, including commercial and open source products, in tabular format for ease of comparison. Most can be found in production use or in active pilot projects in multiple libraries. The next section discusses some additional products or projects that have not yet found active use or that differ somewhat from our definition of discovery interfaces.

AQUABROWSER LIBRARY	
AquaBrowser was the first product in this genre and is the most widely deployed. The technology was developed out of research at the Dutch company BSO Philips Origin conducted by Professor M.M. Chanowski. Medialab Solutions was spun off as a separate company, established to develop and market AquaBrowser to libraries. AquaBrowser was widely adopted by Dutch libraries and has since been marketed internationally (see Figure 2.2). The Library Corporation marketed AquaBrowser from 2004 through 2007. Infor Library and Information Solutions markets AquaBrowser in the United Kingdom. Following the acquisition of Medialab Solutions by R.R. Bowker in June 2007, distribution of the product takes place through multiple channels, including Serials Solutions (academic libraries in North America), Medialab Solutions, Infor Library and Information Solutions, and R.R. Bowker. AquaBrowser's distinctive features include a relevancy-based search engine, faceted navigation, a visually appealing interface, and an interactive word cloud that assists users in exploring related terms found within search results.	
Company	R.R. Bowker (part of CIG): www.bowker.com
	Academic distributor: Serials Solutions (CIG): www.serialssolutions.com
	Europe: Developer: Medialab Solutions, a subsidiary of R.R. Bowker: www.medialab.nl
	United Kingdom: Infor Library and Information Solutions: vubis-smart.com
Web site	www.aquabrowser.com
Software license	Proprietary, closed source software
Price structure	Initial license fee; annual maintenance fee based on size and complexity of library; optional fees for My Discoveries, federated search, etc.
Implementation	Local installation; AquaBrowser Online available as a remotely hosted option for smaller collections
Architecture	
Data workflow model	Harvested metadata from ILS and other repositories
ILS	Works with any major ILS, harvested MARC21, and holdings data; real-time connections for availability and circulation status; in a consortial implementation, can integrate with multiple ILSs
Digital collections	Can be imported into AquaBrowser through any structured file format, including XML, CSV, Microsoft Access, and other SQLs
E-journal content	Optional integration with federated search to address e-journals and other content from external providers
Federated search?	Optional integrated federated search available; WebFeat and 360 Search available through Bowker or Serials Solutions, but will work with other products (e.g., Aston University in Birmingham, England, uses AquaBrowser with Ex Libris MetaLib)
Technology	
Search engine	Proprietary; based on technology developed by Medialab Solutions; performs stemming, fuzzy match, semantic and statistical text analyses
Special requirements	Flash needed for word cloud animations; text-only pages available that do not require Flash, JavaScript, or plug-ins
Features	
Results sorting	Relevancy by default; options for date or alphabetical order by author or title
Faceted browsing	Categories of facets presented on right panel of display; includes item counts on terms; facet categories configurable

▶ Figure 2.2: AquaBrowser at the Queens Borough Public Library in New York

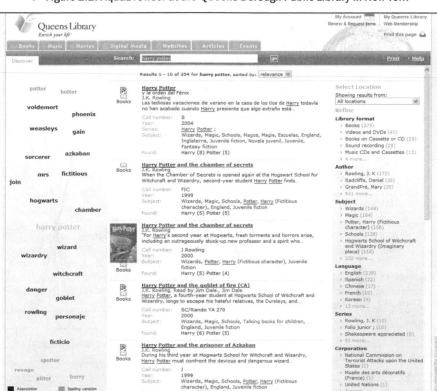

Enriched content	Available through subscription services: cover art, table of contents, summaries, reviews; Syndetic Solutions (a major provider of enriched content owned by R.R. Bowker) available as content for display; Syndetics ICE provides content for indexing to improve discovery
Query recommendations	"Did you mean?" feature offers search suggestions; word cloud presents variants
Social features	My Discoveries component adds user-supplied tags and reviews; option to include tags from LibraryThing for Libraries
Tag clouds	Word cloud to assist users in exploring related terms and concepts
Visual navigation	Visual cloud of associated terms on the left panel of display to help recalculate relevancy or retrieve new search results
Reference Sites	
Total installations	651 libraries as of April 2009; Medialab reports that 80 percent of Dutch public libraries use AquaBrowser as their search interface
Public libraries	Queens Borough Public Library: www.queenslibrary.org Denver Public Library: http://discover.denverlibrary.org

Academic libraries	University of Chicago: http://lens.lib.uchicago.edu
	Oklahoma State University: http://boss.library.okstate.edu
	University of Pittsburgh: http://pittcatplus.pitt.edu
	Harvard University: http://discovery.lib.harvard.edu

Product History

1990: Medialab founded by Professor M.M. Thijs Chanowski as a multimedia research facility in the Dutch company BSO Philips Origin.

2000: Medialab Solutions becomes a separate company to market AquaBrowser

Sept. 2004: The Library Corporation signs an agreement with Medialab to distribute AquaBrowser in the United States and Singapore.

June 2007: R.R. Bowker acquires Medialab Solutions

May 2008: Serials Solutions becomes the distributor for academic libraries

BIBLIOCOMMONS

BiblioCommons, a service offered by a company of the same name, is a hosted discovery interface that emphasizes social networking concepts. In addition to the standard features such as enriched displays, relevancy ranking of results, and faceted navigation, BiblioCommons allows library users to tag or comment on any entry managed within the interface. The product has been involved in the Oakville Public Library in Ontario, Canada, since May 2007 (see Figure 2.3). Major libraries that have since implemented BiblioCommons include the Edmonton Public Library and the Ottawa Public Library in Canada and the Santa Clara Libraries in California.

Company	BiblioCommons
Web site	www.bibliocommons.com
Price structure	Annual subscription service
Implementation	Available as a shared, hosted environment

Architecture

Data workflow model	Based on a model in which data from multiple libraries using the product aggregate together
ILS	Currently operates with the Horizon ILS at Oakville, Ontario

Features

Interface features	Relevancy ranking, cover art display, faceted navigation
Faceted browsing	Facet groups include availability, topics, language, publication data, genre, region, authors, and user-supplied tags
Query recommendations	Ability to select related items through subject heading facets
Social features	Ability to tag and review items
Visual navigation	Visual shelf-browsing tool

Reference Sites

Total installations	1
Public libraries	Oakville Public Library (Canada): www.opl.on.ca

Product History

May 2006: BiblioCommons announced

June 2008: First library puts BiblioCommons into production

▶ Figure 2.3: BiblioCommons at the Oakville Public Library in Ontario, Canada

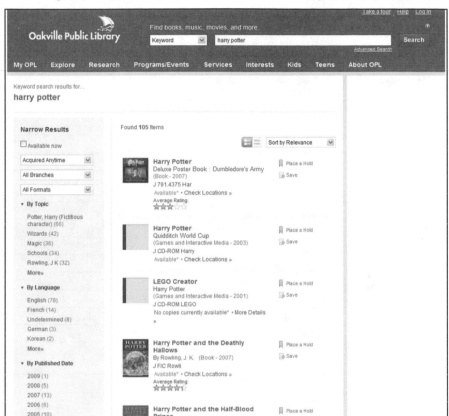

ENCORE
Many types of libraries have adopted Innovative Interfaces' Encore discovery services platform. While the majority of these libraries use Innovative's own Millennium ILS, some libraries that use other ILS products have also chosen Encore. Encore's distinctive features include a simple search box as a starting point, relevancy-ranked results using a proprietary algorithm designed specifically for library content, faceted navigation, a word cloud for related concepts, and virtual shelf browsing (see Figure 2.4). Innovative offers a Query API that gives libraries more open access to the data and functionality of Encore and its underlying ILS.

Company	Innovative Interfaces, Inc.
Web site	www.iii.com/products/encore.shtml http://encoreforlibraries.com
Software license	Proprietary, closed source
Price structure	Software license fee plus annual maintenance and support
Implementation	Locally installed software; hosted version also available

Architecture	
Data workflow model	Harvesting from ILS and other repositories
ILS	Works with all major ILS products
Digital collections	Harvests any repository that offers OAI-PMH
E-journal content	Accessed through harvested content or federated search
Federated search?	Integrates with Innovative's Research Pro and other federated search applications
Technology	
Search engine	Proprietary search engine developed by Innovative Interfaces
Features	
Results sorting	Relevancy based on Right Result, Title, or Date
Faceted browsing	Supported with multiple facet categories with counts of items retrieved upon selection
Enriched content	Supports enriched content from Syndetic Solutions
Social features	User-supplied tags and reviews
Tag clouds	Tag clouds displayed
Visual navigation	Visual shelf-browsing component; visual scroll bar
Reference Sites	
Total installations	170 as of June 2009
Public libraries	Scottsdale Public Library: http://library.ci.scottsdale.az.us
Kent District Library:	www.kdl.org
Academic libraries	Wayne State University: www.lib.wayne.edu
	University of Western Ontario: www.lib.uwo.ca
	Michigan State University: www.lib.msu.edu

▶ Figure 2.4: Encore at the Michigan State University Libraries

Others	Lillian Goldman Law Library, Yale University: http://encore.law.yale.edu

Product History
May 2006: Encore announced by Innovative Interfaces
Oct. 2007: Encore 1.0 released and put into production in 12 libraries
June 2008: Encore 2.0 released
May 2009: Encore 3.0 released

ENDECA PROFIND
Endeca for Libraries is based on the Endeca Information Access Platform, an environment designed to support faceted navigation and relevance-based searching. Endeca does not offer a turnkey product for libraries but rather an environment that can be adapted and customized as a discovery layer interface. Endeca is widely used in the e-commerce sector. North Carolina State University, one of the earliest academic libraries to replace their built-in online catalog with a new discovery interface, based their new system on Endeca technology. Endeca has since been used by a handful of other libraries, including the Phoenix Public Library (see Figure 2.5), the union catalog for the public universities in Florida, a combined catalog of the Research Triangle Library Network, and McMaster University.

Company	Endeca
Web site	www.endeca.com
Software license	Proprietary, closed source
Price structure	Negotiated based on size of collection and other factors
Implementation	Locally installed software; does not offer a library-specific product; some libraries built custom search environments based on Endeca ProFind

Architecture	
Data workflow model	Data harvested from ILS; real-time links back to ILS for current status data; multiple ILSs can be harvested to form combined catalog
ILS	Custom integration by each library; has been used with Unicorn (North Carolina State University), Aleph (Florida Center for Library Automation), Horizon (McMaster University), Carl (Phoenix Public Library), Polaris (Phoenix Public Library), and Millennium (University of North Carolina, Chapel Hill)
Digital collections	Possible given the flexibility of the technology; library implementations to date focus on ILS data
E-journal content	Possible through custom loading and indexing
Federated search?	Through custom programming

Technology	
Search engine	Proprietary search engine developed for Endeca

Features	
Results sorting	Relevancy by default; other sort options available depending on indexing options implemented
Faceted browsing	Specializes in using facets through a technique it calls Guided Navigation
Enriched content	Through custom programming

Query recommendations	Capabilities built into the search engine; implemented through custom programming
Social features	Can be implemented through custom programming
Tag clouds	Can be implemented through custom programming
Visual navigation	Can be implemented through custom programming
Reference Sites	
Public libraries	Used for Web site and catalog by Phoenix Public Library: www.phoenixpubliclibrary.org

▶ Figure 2.5: Endeca at the Phoenix Public Library

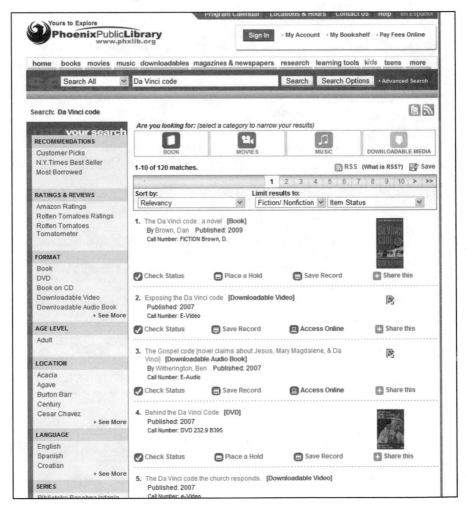

Academic libraries	North Carolina State University: www.lib.ncsu.edu/catalog
	Joint Triangle Research Network (NCSU, Duke University, University of North Carolina Chapel Hill, North Carolina Central University): http://search.trln.org
	McMaster University: http://libcat.mcmaster.ca
	Florida Center for Library Automation (combined catalog of the 11 institutions of the University Libraries of Florida): http://catalog.fcla.edu

Product History
The University of North Carolina State libraries used Endeca to create one of the first discovery interfaces for academic libraries, launched in January 2005.

LS2 PAC

The Library Corporation created the LSC PAC as the first module of an entirely new automation system that will eventually supersede its two current ILS products, Library.Solution and Carl.X. While the company plans to support both of these existing products for the long term, it has begun developing a new platform. The LS2 PAC is part of this new platform and also functions as a new-generation online catalog for both Carl.X and Library.Solution. LS2 PAC uses Flash and other advanced interface technologies. Consistent with the demographics of the company's customer base, LS2 PAC was designed primarily for public libraries. LS2 PAC addresses the content of the ILS and does not aim to expand the scope beyond the traditional online catalog (see Figure 2.6).

Company	The Library Corporation
Web site	www.ls2delivers.com
Software license	Proprietary, closed source
Price structure	License fee plus annual maintenance
Implementation	Locally installed software, harvesting data from the Carl.X or Library.Solution ILS

Architecture	
Data workflow model	Harvesting from ILS; real-time status from ILS
ILS	Operates with The Library Corporation's Library.Solution and Carl.X ILSs
Federated search?	Subscription data integrated into search results through built-in federated search component

Technology	
Search engine	Based on Lucene

Features	
Interface features	Relevancy-ranked results, faceted navigation, autocompletion for search queries, RSS feeds for search results, browsing by genre
Enriched content	Makes thorough use of cover images
Social features	End-user tagging, reviews
Visual navigation	Has a variety of visual navigation features, including the "book river," a stream of book cover images representing items from the library's collection where users can click to display items of interest, and graphical selection tools for material lists such as new titles or best sellers.

▶ Figure 2.6: LS2 PAC at Russell County Public Library

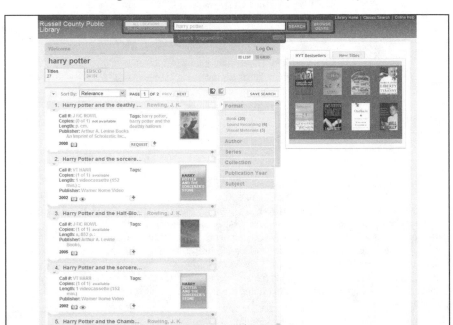

Reference Sites	
Total installations	Purchased by 90 libraries as of June 2009
Public libraries	Shenandoah County Library System: www.shenandoah.co.lib.va.us
	Pasco County Library System: http://pascolibraries.org
Product History	
October 2008: LS2 PAC announced	
November 2008: First installation at Shenandoah County Library System in Virginia	

PRIMO	
Primo, developed by Ex Libris, targets academic and research libraries. Its discovery services rely on a central index populated by the harvesting of content in an OAI model. Ex Libris positions Primo as its strategic end-user interface for its suite of products that include Aleph, Verde, and DigiTool, as well as for its next-gen library automation platform, URM. Primo has also been adopted by many libraries using ILS products from other vendors (see Figure 2.7). The Primo architecture incorporates the ability to connect to the indexes of other compatible discovery systems to provide access to resources beyond that which the library indexes locally. Ex Libris announced in July 2009 a service called Primo Central, a prepopulated index of e-journal content that will be available to libraries using Primo.	
Company	Ex Libris Group
Web site	www.exlibrisgroup.com/category/PrimoOverview
Software license	Proprietary, closed source

Price structure	Initial software licensing fee, annual support and maintenance; cost based on collection size and other factors
Implementation	Locally installed; single library and consortia supported; has a hosted version called Primo Direct

Architecture	
Data workflow model	Harvesting from ILS and other repositories
ILS	Operates with all major ILS products
Digital collections	Can access content from local digital collections or any repository accessible through OAI-PMH
E-journal content	Available through federated search and through "Deep Search," a feature that allows Primo installations to connect through APIs to other compatible indexes (Primo Central, hosted by Ex Libris, will offer a large prepopulated index of articles from a variety of publishers to provide libraries the ability to include large collections of articles in relevancy-ranked search results. Primo Central is planned for beta release by the end of 2009.)
Federated search?	Can be used to search content not in local index; supports only MetaLib, Ex Libris' own federated search product

Technology	
Search engine	Based on Lucene

Features	
Results sorting	Relevance, based on factors tunable by the library
Faceted browsing	Facet groups customizable
Enriched content	Supports a variety of content options: Syndetics ICE, Amazon Web Service, Google Book Search API
Recommendations	An optional bX Recommender service relies on SFX usage data to present related scholarly works
Social features	User-supplied tags and reviews; option for library to approve content prior to posting
Tag clouds	Presented on right panel of record display; used to narrow results; font sizes proportional to number of records represented

Reference Sites	
Total installations	180 by June 2009
Academic libraries	University of Minnesota: www.lib.umn.edu University of Iowa: www.lib.uiowa.edu Emory University: http://discovere.emory.edu New York University: www.bobcat.nyu.edu
Others	British Library: http://searchbeta.bl.uk Royal Library of Denmark: www.kb.dk/en/ext._links/REX

Product History
June 2006: Primo announced with development partner sites: Vanderbilt University, University of Minnesota
May 2007: General release of Primo Version 1
May 2008: General release of Primo Version 2

▶ Figure 2.7: Primo at the University of Iowa Libraries

SIRSIDYNIX ENTERPRISE	
SirsiDynix Enterprise, initially announced in June 2008, uses search engine technology from BrainWare, which specializes in fuzzy match searching. The product primarily addresses the content managed by the ILS and currently supports only the company's own ILS products, including Unicorn. The product is currently positioned as a faceted interface for a library's ILS or for that of a consortium (see Figure 2.8).	
Company	SirsiDynix
Web site	www.sirsidynix.com
Software license	Proprietary, closed source software
Implementation	Current versions available only as software as a service (SaaS); local installations may become possible in later releases
Architecture	
Data workflow model	Data harvested from local ILS to remotely hosted Enterprise installation

ILS	Currently targets SirsiDynix's own products, Symphony and Horizon
Digital collections	Support not mentioned in promotional literature or seen in current implementations
E-journal content	Not addressed
Federated search?	Support for integrated federated expected in future versions
Technology	
Search engine	Based on the GlobalBrain search engine from BrainWare
Features	
Interface features	Faceted browsing, enriched content through Syndetic Solutions, RSS feeds for search results, search suggestions
Reference Sites	
Public libraries	Bedford (IN) Public Library: http://bed.ent.sirsi.net
	Cromaine District Library: http://crom.ent.sirsi.net/vse/app
	Yuma County Library District: http://yuma.ent.sirsi.net/vse/app
Product History	
January–June 2008: SirsiDynix Enterprise announced	
2009: SirsiDynix Enterprise 2.0 released	

▶ Figure 2.8: SirsiDynix Enterprise at the Bedford (IN) Public Library

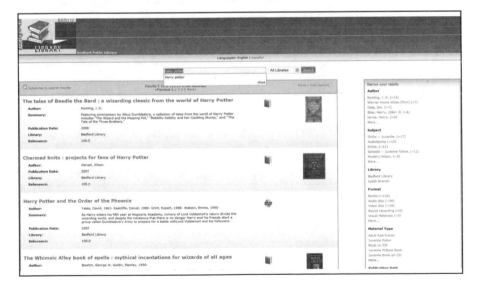

SUMMON	
Summon, announced by Serials Solutions at the ALA Annual conference in January 2009, aims to provide a comprehensive discovery environment including a broad range of electronic content and access to the collection represented in the library's ILS and digital collections (see Figure 2.9). It was launched as a production product in July 2009. Its distinctive features include a massive prepopulated index of preharvested articles from a wide variety of publishers, an API for integrating the search service into other library applications or discovery interfaces, and the ability to limit results to full-text content or to scholarly content.	
Company	Serials Solutions
Web site	www.serialssolutions.com/summon/index.html
Price structure	Annual subscription fee
Implementation	Hosted service; no local software; connectors to ILS systems for real-time status of physical materials
Architecture	
Data workflow model	Consolidated index, hosted by Serials Solutions, that includes large collections of e-journal content provided through agreements with publishers; local ILS content harvested and made available through the library's view of the index
ILS	All major ILSs supported; connectors to ILS will provide real-time access to physical materials
Digital collections	Harvesting model in the library's view of the index
E-journal content	Indexes hosted by Serials Solutions provide access to large collections of harvested content from open access resources and providers including ProQuest, Gale, and many others; initial version of Summon expected to index over 400 million articles
Federated search?	Integrated federated search component allows access to resources not covered in the central index; has two major federated search platforms, 360 Search and WebFeat, which will be merged in 2010
Technology	
Search engine	Lucene
Features	
Interface features	Relevancy-ranked results, faceted navigation
Enriched content	Syndetic Solutions and Syndetics ICE available for enriched content associated with the library's physical inventory
Reference Sites	
Total installations	Initial sites include Grand Valley State University and Hudkersfield University in the United Kingdom
Public libraries	Initially targeted primarily to academic libraries
Academic libraries	None in production, but development partners include Oklahoma State University, Dartmouth College, University of Sydney, University of Liverpool, and University of Calgary
Product History	
July 2009: Product launched	

▶ Figure 2.9: Summon at Grand Valley State University

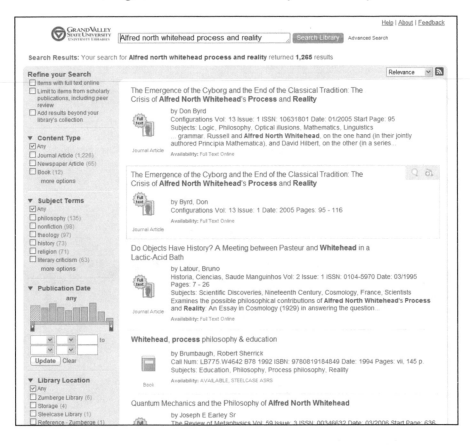

VUFIND	
VuFind, an open source discovery interface initially developed at Villanova University, has gained wide attention as an alternative to the commercially developed products (see Figure 2.10). Because it is open source, VuFind can be populated according to local needs.	
Company	Open source
Web site	www.vufind.org
Software license	General Public License open source license
Price structure	Freely available for downloading and use by any individual or organization
Implementation	Locally installed software
Architecture	
Data workflow model	Data harvesting model
ILS	Operates with any ILS; current implementations include Aleph, Voyager, Virtua, and Unicorn

Digital collections	Can be harvested into the VuFind index
E-journal content	Possible for library to index citation metadata
Federated search?	Possible through local programming
Technology	
Search engine	Based on the Apache Lucene search engine and Apache Solr
Features	
Interface features	Relevancy-ranked search results; online display of item status through AJAX; collection browsing
Reference Sites	
Total installations	More than 20 known; may be additional sites because the software is freely available
Public libraries	Not known to be implemented by any public library

▶ Figure 2.10: VuFind at Villanova University

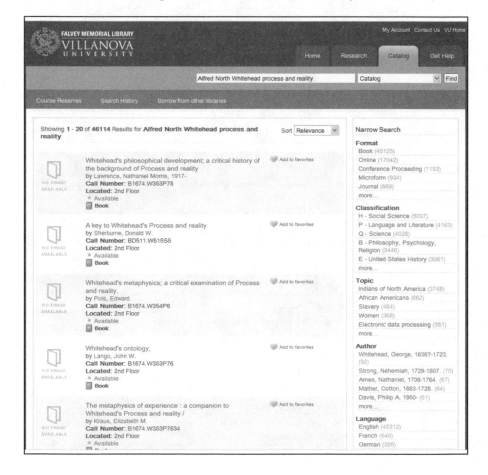

Academic libraries	Villanova University: http://library.villanova.edu/Find
	Consortium of Academic and Research Libraries in Illinois: http://vufind-beta.carli.illinois.edu
	Colorado State University: http://discovery.library.colostate.edu
Others	National Library of Australia: http://catalogue.nla.gov.au

Product History
July 2007: Villanova University announced VuFind
May 2008: National Library of Australia launched catalog based on VuFind

WORLDCAT LOCAL
OCLC's WorldCat Local, a subscription service designed to replace a library's local online catalog, is positioned as a discovery environment that also offers access to large collections of e-journal content and to a library's digital collection (see Figure 2.11). WorldCat Local searches all of the material in WorldCat.org, a massive bibliographic database of 137 million records, sorting results so that materials in the user's home library appear first in the list. This broad searching technique allows the user to discover what material exists even if it isn't held locally. WorldCat Local offers interlibrary loan and direct consortial borrowing capabilities that facilitate the delivery of materials not available in the local library. Libraries can brand their view of WorldCat Local with their own logos and presentation styles. OCLC has recently made an agreement with EBSCO to include the article-level metadata from EBSCOhost in search results to provide access to e-journal and periodical content. WorldCat Local subscribers can also include digital resources from repository platforms such as CONTENTdm into their search environment.

Company	OCLC
Web site	www.oclc.org
Software license	Subscription service
Price structure	Annual subscription fee, based on size of library and other factors
Implementation	No locally installed software; all access through Web browser; involves connectors to local ILS for real-time status

Architecture	
Data workflow model	Based on the library's holdings as represented by WorldCat.org; OCLC will perform a reclamation process that synchronizes WorldCat.org with the library's local ILS
ILS	WorldCat Local currently operates with any major ILS; OCLC has announced extensions to WorldCat Local that will also provide automation services for circulation, acquisitions, and license management, eventually obviating the need for a library to operate a local ILS
Digital collections	Local collections can be integrated to WorldCat Local through harvesting into WorldCat.org; OCLC also owns CONTENTdm, which many libraries use for managing local digital collections, and provides services related to making this content available through WorldCat.org
E-journal content	WorldCat Local provides access to e-journal content through indexing large collections in WorldCat.org. The pilot version of WorldCat Local included about 30 million articles in its ArticleFirst resource. OCLC has recently formed an agreement with EBSCO to index all the article content available in EBSCOhost, which will be available to libraries that subscribe

	to both WorldCat Local and EBSCOhost. OCLC is pursuing agreements with other providers to further expand the article content available to WorldCat Local subscribers.
Federated search?	For e-journal and other content not represented in WorldCat.org, OCLC has recently integrated federated search into WorldCat Local, based on technology licensed from Index Data.
Technology	
Search engine	OCLC's proprietary Find search engine
Server environment	Requires no local server
Client requirements	Any Web browser
Features	
Interface features	Relevancy-ranked results, query recommendations
Faceted browsing	Facet categories include author, format, publication year, genre, audience, language, and subjects
Enriched content	Integrated image art provided
Reference Sites	
Academic libraries	University of Washington (www.lib.washington.edu)
Product History	
April 2007: WorldCat Local announced	
June 2008: Partnership with Index Data to add federated search	
April 2009: OCLC announces WorldCat Local quick start and its plans to deliver full automation functionality through WorldCat Local	

▶ Figure 2.11: WorldCat Local at the University of Washington

Related Projects and Products

This section considers some of the other products associated with the genre of discovery interfaces. These may not fit our broad definition of a discovery interface or have not reached the stage of implementation.

eXtensible Catalog

The eXtensible Catalog (XC) project has been funded by the Andrew W. Mellon Foundation to explore the requirements of a next-gen library interface and to create software that implements the concepts. The University of Rochester River Campus Libraries leads the development with the involvement of a variety of partners. The Mellon Foundation awarded $283,000 for the initial planning and conceptual development. It awarded a second grant of $749,000 in October 2007. Following a period of internal development, components of the XC software were released in March 2009. XC will initially target academic libraries. As of June 2009, XC has not been implemented as a production catalog by any library.

The design of XC will involve an interface delivered in five modules. The interface itself will be created using the open source Drupal content management system through a component called the Drupal Toolkit. The project released an OAI Toolkit and an NCIP Toolkit for the extraction of data from target repositories and real-time interactions with the existing ILS. A Metadata Services Toolkit will provide services for normalizing and enhancing metadata derived from each target repository. This module will implement authority control and apply FRBR groupings and other transformations to improve the way that the metadata support discovery. A Learning Management Toolkit will support integration of library services with courseware and learning management systems. The software produced in the XC project will be made available as open source through the MIT License. For more information on the eXtensible Catalog, see www.extensiblecatalog .org.

Blacklight

The Digital Initiatives unit of the University of Virginia libraries developed an open source discovery layer application called Blacklight that has begun to attract interest. Originally created in support of NINES (Nineteenth-century Scholarship Online), the software has been adapted and extended to perform the functions on a new-generation online catalog. Like many other discovery products, Blacklight uses Apache Lucene and Solr components. Blacklight is distinctive in its use of Ruby on Rails as the programming framework to deliver a customized interface. In addition to MARC records, it has been designed to operate with many other XML metadata formats, including TEI (Text Encoding Initiative), EAD (Encoded Archival Description), and GDMS (General Descriptive Modeling Scheme), all of which are widely used at the University of Virginia. One of the key goals of Blacklight involves producing a faceted discovery interface that works well with mixed metadata representing different types of collections. Principals involved in the development of Blacklight include Bess Sadler and Erik Hatcher.

The University of Libraries has implemented Blacklight as the basis of a new interface for its online catalog, currently available as a beta test alternative (see http://virgobeta.lib.virginia.edu). Blacklight is an open source application licensed under the Apache 2.0 License.

National Library of Australia Single Business Discovery Service

I noted earlier that the National Library of Australia has implemented VuFind as the default interface for its Voyager-based automation environment. The Voyager ILS represents only one of many of the information resources created and maintained by this national library. In addition to the print collections represented in Voyager, the library creates and maintains separate collections of images, digitized newspapers, maps, and music and has archived Australian Web sites since 1996. In one of the more interesting and ambitious efforts in the discovery layer arena, the National Library of Australia recently completed the Single Business Discovery Service (SBDS) prototype. SBDS uses Apache Lucene and Solr as its search engine, is programmed in Java, and uses MySQL for record clustering and other housekeeping functions.

As discovery interfaces increasingly need to address diverse types of collections and very large-scale quantities of metadata and full-text content, this project will be worth following closely. The SBDS prototype is available at http://sbdsproto.nla.gov.au.

EBSCO Discovery Service

EBSCO has announced plans to offer a discovery service similar to WorldCat Local and Summon based on large prepopulated indexes of e-journals and other electronic content. I noted earlier that OCLC struck an agreement with EBSCO to provide e-journal indexing in WorldCat Local. This reciprocal agreement also provides EBSCO with access to WorldCat.org records. The article indexing already present in EBSCOhost, plus the access to WorldCat.org records, form the basis of the new EBSCO Discovery Service. EBSCO indicates that it has made agreements with many other publishers and providers of e-journals and other electronic content to expand the material available through this service. The EBSCO Discovery Service, as currently described, will involve harvesting data from the library's ILS and digital repositories, which will combine with the index maintained by EBSCO that includes large collections of e-content and print material to produce the ability to search all the key components of a library's collection.

The company also offers EBSCOhost integrated search, planned for release in June 2009, which folds a federated search engine into EBSCOhost, allowing a library to provide access to non-EBSCO resources through the same interface. The EBSCO Discovery Interface will have the ability to use this federated search technology to extend access to any resources not preharvested into its core indexes.

The EBSCO Discovery Service is slated for release by the end of 2009. For more information, see www.ebscohost.com/thisTopic.php ?marketID=1&topicID=1245.

New Online Catalogs as Next-Gen

The dominant trend today involves libraries acquiring a discovery interface that replaces the online catalog module of their ILS. Some products buck this trend, building into the online catalog module of an ILS many of the interfacing and indexing features that have become standard fare in the genre of discovery layer products. These online catalogs continue to be tied to the ILS, so they don't necessarily expand the scope of search but they do provide a modern interface.

The Web-based online catalog modules of the two major open source ILS products Evergreen and Koha as well as that of the Polaris Integrated Library System from Polaris all include many of the interface conventions seen in the discovery layer products. Each offers relevancy-ranked result listings, facets for narrowing search results, and cover art to enhance visual appeal.

Because these online catalogs remain tied to the ILS, they do not require the same data workflows as apply to those that operate as independent discovery layer products. They use proprietary connections with the integrated system rather than rely on metadata harvesting and Web services or deep-linking mechanisms for real-time availability and status for displayed items. Although these integrated online catalogs remain simpler to maintain, they do not expand the scope of discovery beyond the content of the ILS, which we have seen as an increasingly important concern.

The ability of these three products to satisfy much of the concerns addressed by discovery layer products is reinforced by the observation that few, if any, of the libraries operating these ILS products have implemented a discovery product to replace their integrated online catalog. Note that the Phoenix Public Library implemented an Endeca-based Web site and discovery environment with its previous Carl ILS and maintained that environment as it switched to the Polaris ILS.

It's also the case that the online catalogs are not designed to operate as discovery interfaces for use with other ILS products. Some libraries may migrate to an ILS product to gain a more modern interface, but this involves a larger process than implementing a new discovery layer interface with their existing environment.

Helpful Tools

The discovery products covered in this book provide a complete solution to delivering a new interface for accessing a library's collection. Some other products are available that offer specialized functions that can be integrated either with a discovery layer product or with a traditional online catalog.

LibraryThing for Libraries

LibraryThing for Libraries provides socially supplied tags and reviews for library catalogs. LibraryThing offers a service for managing personal book collections. This extremely popular service helps individuals, or even small libraries, organize their collections. One of the key features involves assigning tags and reviews shared throughout the community of LibraryThing users. Users can assign existing tags or create new ones as needed. This growing body of user-assigned tags represents one of the most powerful organizational features of LibraryThing. A related product, LibraryThing for Libraries, exploits the tags, reviews, and other user-supplied data in LibraryThing for integration in library catalogs. By matching with ISBNs or other identifiers, a library can populate each of the records in its catalog with socially created information to supplement its formal cataloging. Social features such as user tags and reviews can be unsatisfying until a sufficient quantity accumulates. LibraryThing for Libraries addresses this issue by seeding a library interface with a critical mass of data that otherwise would take many years to build (see Figure 2.12).

R.R. Bowker owns a portion of LibraryThing and exclusively distributes the LibraryThing for Library service (www.librarything.com/forlibraries). The optional My Discoveries social component of AquaBrowser relies on the tags and the reviews supplied through LibraryThing for Libraries.

ChiliFresh

The ChiliFresh Review Engine (www.chilifresh.com) is another service that supplies social content to library resources. Through a plug-in, li-

▶ Figure 2.12: Millennium Catalog at the Danbury (CT) Public Library with Related Works and Tags Supplied through LibraryThing for Libraries

brary catalogs allow patrons to submit reviews on any material viewed from the catalog. The reviews go into a repository shared by all libraries subscribing to ChiliFresh. Once an item has been reviewed by a patron in one library, all subscribers can then view it. Libraries can choose to suppress reviews until they have been vetted.

ChiliFresh can be integrated into both traditional online catalogs and discovery layer products. SirsiDynix, for example, offers ChiliFresh as an optional add-in to its Enterprise discovery service (see Figure 2.13).

▶ LAY THE GROUNDWORK

The implementation of a next-gen library catalog represents one of the most important aspects of a library's automation strategy. The product that you put forward will not only represent one of the key experiences of the library by its users, but it will also impact almost all library staff members. Such a project involves a major undertaking and will provide great opportunity for a library to exercise its best organizational skills related to planning, decision making, change management, and communications.

▶ Figure 2.13: ChiliFresh Review Engine Embedded in the Greater Manchester Integrated Library Cooperative System Polaris Catalog

Here, I explore some of the steps involved in planning for the implementation of a new discovery interface. I'll review some of the organizational processes that should contribute to a more successful project. All libraries differ in how they approach large projects, so I must acknowledge a wide variety of alternatives in the ways that library organizations operate. Processes involving decision making, communications, project management, and the like will be handled differently by each library. This section doesn't presume any given style of management but attempts only to highlight a few of the more relevant activities involved in changing to a discovery interface.

The organizational aspects of a consortium implementation will be even more complex. The increased number of stakeholders will likely increase the difficulty of decision making and communications. The more dissimilar the members of the consortium, the harder it will be to arrive at a common vision and determine a mutually agreeable solution. Yet, the larger body of resources that can be addressed by a discovery interface adds tremendous value to the users of the system. One of the major trends in library automation involves cooperative services where libraries pool their efforts and resources to increase the value of their services to their users while decreasing their individual costs.

One of the major trends playing out in library automation involves separating the public interface from the tools that the library staff use in their own work. This approach allows the library to improve its virtual presence without the massive level of effort involved in an ILS migration.

The library's public-facing product generally has more to do with its success than the software it uses to provide automation support for its staff. While the ILS, electronic resource management systems, and other automation tools impact aspects of staff productivity, these make little difference to library patrons. Given these competing priorities, many libraries feel greater urgency to make improvements in the systems that involve direct interaction with library users and defer major replacements of the software used internally by library staff.

It's vital to begin laying the groundwork at the earliest possible stage as the library embarks on investigating any new interface for its patrons. The implementation of a next-gen catalog touches almost every aspect of the library—behind the scenes, inside the library, and especially for the library's Web presence. But how does the library arrive at the decision that it needs to make a change?

In most cases, the inception begins with informal conversations. If the ideas resonate with larger groups or with library administrators, a more organized set of discussions will take place in committees, workgroups, or other channels within the library's organization. The process of turning an idea into a sanctioned project will involve gaining the support of the library's governing body, and its success will depend on building support among a broad base of key players throughout the library.

Gaining support to launch a project may require the gathering of data to substantiate the need and provide evidence that a new discovery interface will result in an improvement. The data pointing to problems with the status quo may take a variety of forms:

- ► An accumulation of complaints from library users
- ► Results of a satisfaction survey
- ► Observations of patron frustration by library staff
- ► Analysis of use logs of the current online catalog that indicate high numbers of unsuccessful search sessions
- ► Statistics that demonstrate that segments of the library's collection are underused

While it's feasible to gather anecdotal and statistical evidence that the current online catalog may no longer be the ideal interface, it may be more difficult to demonstrate that one of the new discovery interfaces will resolve the issues. The experiences that other libraries have with some of these products may help make the case. It's important to have strong evidence that a proposed project to implement a new discovery interface warrants the expenditure of time and resources in the context of other competing priorities.

Build a Common Vision

Because the transition to a new search environment involves practically every aspect of the library, it's important that all library personnel understand what the move aims to accomplish. First, clarify the problems that exist with the library's current search environment and how the new product will address these issues. To the extent possible, gather data that demonstrate the points of dissatisfaction. If part of the reason involves providing better access to underutilized electronic resources, then make this goal clear.

Also keep in mind that the library can offer multiple interfaces. It's not realistic to expect any given search tool to serve all possible needs.

The native interfaces will continue to be useful. It's common, for example, for a library to use a new discovery interface but to continue offering the traditional library catalog as an advanced search option. Likewise, as users see journal articles within a results list, they may want to shift to the native interface of an e-content provider to work more in depth with that material.

Manage Change

The transition to a new search interface will bring widespread changes throughout the library, but it will affect some groups of staff more than others. Carefully preparing for all aspects of the change will pay off through increased buy-in and hopefully decreased frustration.

If your library has exceptional difficulties with navigating through the changes that will inevitably emanate from the project, then it might be necessary to undertake a change management exercise. Consider using a facilitator, consultant, or in-house expert to guide the library through the process.

Library staff members are more likely to rally around projects that they believe will improve the library, even if it means change. Making a convincing argument that a new discovery tool will make a positive impact will go a long way toward overcoming resistance to change.

One of the greatest points of anxiety may involve what will stay the same and what will change. In most cases the implementation of the new search environment will not mean dismantling the current ILS. Do not take for granted that staff will understand what will or will not change unless it is specifically and clearly communicated.

Work toward Consensus

Begin building consensus about moving to a next-gen library catalog early in the consideration phase. As the library begins to investigate the possibility of replacing its long-standing library catalog, it should begin the process of engaging staff members. It's never too early to begin enlisting support, identifying pockets of resistance, and addressing legitimate concerns. It's unrealistic to think that 100 percent of library staff will be supportive, but all individuals should feel that their concerns have been heard and addressed and that they have had a voice in the process.

It's important that all library staff fully understand the goals that the new product intends to address. These products will be used by library patrons. Library staff members have much different needs and may not see these next-gen catalogs as an improvement for their own work. Be clear that the interfaces upon which they rely for their work will remain unchanged as the library presents a new search environment for patrons.

Establish Communications Channels

It's essential that everyone involved receives adequate information and has ample opportunities to provide input. Begin the dialogue at the earliest possible phase of the project, even when the idea is just brewing. The collective knowledge of the personnel throughout the library represents a great resource that can be tapped to great advantage if the channels are put into place to allow all individuals to share their knowledge and opinions. While it's great to have champions that spearhead the initiative, it's important that interest and involvement not be limited to a small contingent.

Each library organization will have its distinct methods of communication among its personnel. Hopefully, good communication channels already exist in the library so that it's not necessary to create an entirely new infrastructure for the project. Let's briefly examine some effective ways to communicate.

Broadcast your information widely. Some information may need to be distributed to all, or large subsets, of the library personnel. E-mail distribution lists fill this need but should be used judiciously. A prolific volume of messages can be counterproductive. It's also important for each message to be concise and to the point. Long and complex explanations may overwhelm the key points to some readers. Convey the key message and provide pointers to more detailed information.

Provide information on demand. In addition to broadcast messages, it's important to create documentation that explains the processes underway and any relevant information regarding the product, local implementation details, and any other relevant content. Again, the vehicle for this content will vary depending on established infrastructure but might include a library staff intranet, a project wiki, a blog, or some other collaborative environment. Be sure that all the information is written down coherently and made available to the widest possible audience.

One of the pitfalls of communication involves placing the information some place not generally frequented by library personnel. If the content is in an obscure area with a new password requirement, for example, some staff will not go there. Information should remain within the standard communication infrastructure provided for library staff.

Projects such as this one may prompt the library to expand this infrastructure, but avoid creating a new information repository. While the project may be a major focus for a few key players, it's one of many ongoing concerns for most personnel and needs to be part of the broader fabric of communication.

Allocate Adequate Resources

The implementation of a new discovery environment is a major undertaking and will require a significant investment in resources. This section reviews some key resources you need to have.

First, adequate **funding and availability of key personnel** are necessary to success. Without sufficient financial resources, all your other resources will suffer. Using a product delivered through SaaS will mean fewer demands on technology personnel and no need to purchase new computer hardware because there will be no servers to maintain locally. The annual subscription fee will represent a larger portion of the project costs because it subsumes a variety of hardware, software, and personnel costs borne by the service provider. Libraries that lack adequate in-house technical expertise may find the SaaS option especially attractive.

Libraries that choose a locally implemented product will naturally need to purchase the servers and other technical infrastructure. The installation and maintenance of this equipment will add an incremental allocation of effort to IT personnel.

The **hardware resources** will also vary according to the size and complexity of the implementation and the level of redundancy required. It's not unusual to separate functional components across different physical servers. Database, search engine, and Web components, for example, might each operate on its own dedicated hardware to ensure high performance of the overall system with large data sets expected to sustain heavy levels of use.

The **technical resources** needed for a locally installed product will vary. Some vendors offer a turnkey approach whereby the equipment is housed in the data center of the library, but the vendor performs all the technical work, including installation, configuration, and ongoing maintenance. A software-only implementation will require much more involvement from the library's technical personnel. The amount of technical work increases according to the complexity of data manipulations or major customizations of the interface.

The metadata created by the library's **technical services** units power the search and display of the library's collection. The new interfaces often use the metadata in different ways than the native online catalog bundled with the ILS. The knowledge of metadata and the skills of organizing information will play a valuable role. The library will want to tap the expertise of its technical services staff as it works through issues involving the presentation of facets, relevancy tuning, grouping of records through FRBR, and a myriad of other issues that involve metadata.

The metadata specialists who work on the digital projects that will be subsumed within a discovery environment will also be involved with the new interface. One of the major challenges in creating a resource that indexes content from diverse collections is consistent treatment of metadata and balancing indexing techniques to ensure representative search results.

Reference and other public services staff deal with the library's interfaces continuously. The tools must be adequate for both the general needs of library users and the more rigorous demands of retrieving information to reference questions and conducting in-depth, comprehensive research. When implementing a new environment, reference staff will need to become familiar with its behavior at the earliest possible stage. Reference librarians have deep expertise in search strategies and information retrieval that can be tapped to ensure that the new discovery environment lives up to its potential.

If your library offers **bibliographic instruction** sessions to students, engage the teaching personnel at the earliest phase. The next-gen catalog products may lend themselves to different types of search strategies compared to what may have been taught with the traditional catalog. It takes time to revise the content of the bibliographic instruction curriculum and any handouts or other materials. The lead time for preparation for bibliographic instruction may be longer than for other parts of the library.

The **personnel in the information technology department or systems office** bear much of the load in the implementation and operation of a next-gen library interface. The level of work will vary tremendously depending on whether the product will be installed locally or if it will be remotely hosted. Local installations will involve setting up one or more new servers and installing and configuring software. The most complex work, however, involves data and indexing. In most cases, setting up a new discovery environment involves extracting data from the ILS and other information repositories in the library and loading them into the next-gen catalog. This process requires detailed knowledge on the procedures for exporting data from the current ILS, which will include the full database of MARC records, and may also involve procedures to associate location, holdings, and item information with the bibliographic records as they are extracted. The process may also involve export of authority records and linking them with corresponding bibliographic records. The transfer of records from the ILS to the new catalog may be as simple as running a script or report that is built into the system, or it may involve detailed and complex programming.

Your **Web site developers** need to be involved. Next-gen catalogs will likely result in large changes in the way that the library delivers information through its Web site. Much of the organization of the library's existing site may hinge on assumptions that will no longer apply. The library should be prepared for at least some changes to its Web site as it makes the transition.

One of the main issues on library Web sites concerns the search box and what content it addresses. It's common to have a search box that allows users to find content within the Web site. In the library context, however, the search box is more often directed toward the material in its collections. Users will not necessarily understand the difference between "Search this site" and "Search the catalog." It's better if the contents of the Web site can be indexed within the discovery interface, eliminating the need for a separate search facility.

In most cases, the library will want its discovery environment to adapt to the look and feel of its broader Web presence. The developers of the Web site may be of great assistance in working with the style sheets and other design elements.

▶ SELECT AND PROCURE A DISCOVERY INTERFACE

Once the library has made a decision to go forward with the project, the process of selecting specific products begins. The abundance of options makes the selection process challenging.

The choices involve not just selecting among competing products but also making major conceptual decisions about what constitutes an ideal discovery environment. Decisions regarding open source product versus licensing a commercial solution, locally installed software versus vendor-hosted services, and single-library or consortial implementation should be resolved prior to the initiation of formal procurement.

The procurement process will also vary according to prevailing business procedures and existing business relationships in place in the library. Some libraries operate with organizations that require a formal competitive process with strict procedures for all major purchases. Others allow more informal arrangements. Some organizations that normally require competitive bids will allow the purchase of additional products from a company already established as a major supplier.

If the library already does business with a company that offers a next-gen catalog and is pleased with that relationship, then it might be inclined to avoid the overhead of a full-blown competitive procurement. For many organizations, a **sole-source procurement** radically shortens the timeframe. Vendors will often offer significant discounts when a library as an existing customer purchases additional products. This route bypasses many of the time-consuming steps involved in a formal procurement.

Even if the library is inclined to go with a sole-source purchase, it will want to informally evaluate the full spectrum of options. The essential process of due diligence will either confirm the next-gen product from the library's incumbent vendor as reasonable or clarify the need to open the process to other vendors.

The **competitive procurement** process has a number of steps. Many libraries operate in a business environment that prescribes specific rules to follow when making all major purchases, but the specific rules will vary among organizations. Some libraries will issue a Request for Information to identify qualified systems, and others may develop a Request for Proposal that explains the exact functionality required with the expectation of eliciting formal proposals from vendors, including a full accounting of costs.

The **Request for Information** (RFI) is a document that describes in general terms the characteristics of the product that the library intends to purchase, the features desired, and all relevant information about the library. The library will submit the RFI to a broad set of vendors known to offer products within the scope specified. The RFI should elicit responses from the vendors that provide product details beyond those available in their promotional literature. The response to an RFI may include nonbinding pricing, proposed product options, hardware prerequisites, and other information necessary for the library to give serious consideration to the product.

The **Request for Proposal** (RFP) is a procurement document that specifies the formal requirements that a product must offer to be considered for purchase. An RFP presents detailed questions about the product, the company, and the support options and usually requests a full pricing proposal. Developing an RFP requires considerable knowledge about the product involved. Some libraries issue an RFI in advance of an RFP as part of the information-gathering process. Once the RFP has been completed, it will be distributed to a set of qualified vendors. The RFP will specify the date by which proposals must be submitted and the required components of a response. When the date for opening the RFP arrives, the library begins the evaluation of the proposals and will select the preferred vendor. Once selected, a negotiation process will commence that results in a formal contract and final pricing.

It's possible, however, that none of the proposals will meet the requirements specified in the RFP, and the process concludes without selecting a vendor. If no qualified vendor emerges, the library may need to revise the RFP or consider an alternative process for moving forward.

The full RFP process may take as long as a year from developing the procurement documents to completing a contract. Given the long timeframe, libraries may prefer a more expedient approach if allowable. While installing a new discovery environment ranks as a major endeavor, it may be below the threshold that requires a formal procurement process for some organizations.

One of the pitfalls of the RFP process involves the tendency to specify features expected in so much detail that it limits some products that would accomplish the larger goals but in different ways. With a product genre such as discovery interfaces that is evolving rapidly, it's important to write procurement documents in such a way as to be open to new products that may take a different approach to accomplish the functionality. To the extent possible, a library should express the broader vision of what it hopes to accomplish with its next-gen catalog, allowing for a variety of innovative solutions. A process that defines a static set of features may not be successful at identifying creative alternatives.

Open Source versus Proprietary

Open source products do not necessarily fit within the usual procurement process. It's possible to implement an open source discovery product using only in-house personnel and no external vendor.

A discovery interface project based on an open source software will involve a much different planning process than one based on a commercial product. Libraries interested in an open source discovery product will need technical personnel capable of executing a relatively complex set of tasks, ranging from downloading the software from its repository, installing the software and all its prerequisites, configuring and customizing it, and populating its indexes. As noted, these products generally require extracting data from the library's ILS and other information repositories—another rather technically complex task. In general, going with an open source discovery product will require more in-house technical expertise and the allocation of more library personnel resources relative to purchasing a commercial product where most of these activities can be offloaded to the vendor.

Some libraries may have sufficient technical ability to experiment with an open source discovery interface before deciding among the open source and commercial alternatives. Setting up an open source product will give the library some firsthand experience with this type of product. The library can see how its data perform in a relevancy-based search environment with faceted navigation. Even if the library ultimately decides to purchase a commercial product, much of the effort involved in setting up the prototype can be repurposed. Data extraction routines, for example, established for the prototype may need only minor adjustments to be applied to the commercial product.

Some libraries may want to use an open source product even though they do not have in-house technical personnel. A number of companies have emerged that provide professional ILS implementation and support services. Such products include Koha, Evergreen, and OPALS. Similar arrangements may likewise emerge for the open source discovery products, although most of the implementations to date have been accomplished primarily through internal resources.

▶ FOLLOW A PROCESS BASED ON USER-CENTERED DESIGN

As a genre of products created for libraries, these systems must embody a very strong level of usability. One well-established process for creating a usable interface is called User-Centered Design, of which

Donald Norman was an early proponent. The fundamental consideration in User-Centered Design is how the user will interact with the system. While developed as a general model for all kinds of products, the process has been especially prominent in the development of Web-based resources. Some of the main concepts involved include considering the needs of the user from the earliest stages of product development, having a thorough understanding of its potential users, and following a participatory process that involves the users.

How libraries approach usability will differ depending on whether they are implementing an existing product or whether they are involved in designing the interface. Because the discovery interface targets library patrons, it's their needs that should drive the selection, configuration, and/or development of the interface. Those who work in libraries come with a set of expectations for an information interface that may cloud how they anticipate the shape of an interface designed for patrons. Actively involving patrons in all stages of the process helps ensure that the product implemented better suits its need and that it will find a higher level of acceptance once launched.

In the majority of cases, the library will be implementing an existing product, limiting the opportunity that the library will have to impact its general design. A process based on the principles of User-Centered Design can then come into play during its selection and configuration. It's important not to underutilize end users in the process of launching a new interface and in the decisions made about its placement, design, and operation. Gather verbal comments through focus groups and data from more structured usability exercises by observing users as they work through defined tasks with each candidate product.

One helpful exercise includes usability studies that benchmark the performance of the library's existing search tools versus each of the candidates under consideration. While the scope of these products may differ relative to the inclusion of different formats of materials, it should be possible to devise test scenarios that expose the performance of each of the tools as experienced by actual users.

The implementation of a discovery interface, depending on the product selected, will involve a number of configuration decisions. The options of the elements that can be changed through configuration vary from among the products. Some of the possible decisions include the categories of facets to present; the metadata fields to populate each facet; the indexing rules; the factors to determine relevancy rankings; the selection, positioning, and labeling of elements of brief and full record lists; and the placement of the search box and other components of the discovery interface throughout the library's and its institution's Web presence. As the team working through the configuration of the interface faces each of these decisions, data derived from systematic end-user participation provides important input.

As the library seeks input from its users regarding discovery interface issues, it should consider the differences among each of its segments. In an academic environment, the information needs and preferences regarding interface styles may differ among students, faculty, and support staff. Even within the student community, undergraduate, graduate, residential, and distance students will have different perspectives.

While the main discussion here involves the discovery interface as a purchased product, some libraries may want to design and create their own. This would be an enormous task but also a great opportunity to work with the library's own users to hone an interface optimized for their information needs and functional preferences. Those taking on this more involved endeavor will have the opportunity to follow a process of User-Centered Design that informs the fundamental shape of the system rather than the more limited set of options open to those who acquire a delivered product.

The fundamental goal of the planning and procurement phase of the project is to identify and acquire the product that best matches the vision that the library has formed of the experience it wants to offer to its users. The product needs to offer a rich set of features to users and to fit within the resources that the library has or can acquire in terms of both money and people. The groundwork laid in this planning stage should return good results as the library moves forward with implementation, the focus of our next chapter.

▶3

IMPLEMENTATION

- ▶ **Integrate the Discovery Interface with the ILS**
- ▶ **Extract Data from the ILS**
- ▶ **Import Data into the Discovery Interface**
- ▶ **Establish Real-Time Interactions**
- ▶ **Provide for Ongoing Synchronization**
- ▶ **Load Content from Other Repositories**
- ▶ **Be Aware of Cataloging and Metadata Issues**
- ▶ **Integrate Article-Level Content**
- ▶ **Include Enriched Content**
- ▶ **Plan the Practical Aspects of Implementation**
- ▶ **Monitor and Maintain the System**
- ▶ **Keep Abreast of Emerging Trends**

Once your library has made the decision to implement a new discovery interface, the hard work begins. The specific tasks involved will vary depending on a myriad of circumstances. Open source or proprietary? Locally installed or remotely hosted? Each of these options will play a role in what tasks need to be accomplished and which may either be not needed or will be performed by the vendor supplying the software or the service.

This chapter will present in general terms the tasks involved in implementing a new discovery interface. It provides a broad outline of the activities that need to be accomplished. The specific procedures for your project will vary according to the ILS used, the other information repositories that will populate the discovery interface, and the metadata schemes involved.

As discussed in previous chapters, the discovery interface does not manage data independently; it relies on importing metadata from external resources. The discovery product indexes the metadata and other content derived from these repositories to support end-user searching and access to the materials described. At a minimum, implementation will involve harvesting data from the ILS, with some mechanism for real-time interactions to display current status and for patron services such as renewals and holds. A library may also plan to populate its discovery environment with content held in its digital collections, institutional repository, or other specialized resources. There should also be some provision for access to the library's collection of e-journals.

► INTEGRATE THE DISCOVERY INTERFACE WITH THE ILS

One of the essential elements of implementing a discovery interface is to integrate it with the existing ILS. While discovery interfaces aim to provide access to a broad range of resources, the content managed within the ILS represents the most critical collections that will need to be transferred. The integration of the discovery interface with the ILS will involve a mass transfer of data, keeping the data in sync, and a number of ongoing interactions.

The typical arrangement separates the discovery from the automation systems used by library personnel for cataloging, circulation, acquisitions, and other routine activities. This tactic means that the ILS will be used for the ongoing maintenance of the database that describes the library's collection and that the discovery interface will need to continually receive updates. An accurate representation of the data in the ILS and ongoing synchronization account for some of the most complex and challenging aspects of a discovery interface implementation.

The OPAC module within the ILS takes advantage of its position as a component within a broader system. It has direct access to each of the databases that comprise the integrated system through its internal proprietary channels. As a module of an integrated system, the OPAC can easily draw from and update any of the data stores, proprietary programming, and other features to deliver its functionality. The new discovery products, on the other hand, operate without access to the internal workings of the ILS. Rather, they must rely on extracting data from the ILS as needed via a set of generalized protocols, conventions, and other techniques that require real-time interactions with the ILS.

It's generally expected that any of the discovery products will be able to search the resources managed within the ILS, replete with up-to-date information regarding the current location and status of any given item. For any given title, the discovery interface needs to display which branches hold copies and which are on the shelf or checked out. These data, of course, change constantly and quickly become out of date. To present reliable status information, these data elements must be reharvested and synchronized very frequently or presented through a real-time look-up service. Some discovery environments that rely on harvesting status data synchronize hourly and some even more frequently. Harvesting status data makes it possible to create related filters in the discovery interface such as excluding materials charged out and therefore not currently available. This approach also makes it possible to list approximate status data on a result list without having to poll the underlying ILS for each item. Real-time interactions between the discovery environment and the ILS involve more behind-the-scenes processing overhead but have the obvious advantages of currency and accuracy. Some products use both the harvested status data and real-time look-ups to gain the benefits of both techniques.

Personalized patron services represent the most complex area of interaction between the ILS and the discovery interface. The online catalog module of any respectable ILS offers the ability for patrons to sign in to their account, view items currently checked out, place renewals, make requests to have materials held that are checked out to others, pay fines, request materials owned by other members of a consortium, and be notified when the library acquires new materials within a specified area of interest.

Within the ILS, these services take advantage of a variety of internal databases and proprietary functionality. The bibliographic and item-specific databases and the internal patron files play a role in these services, as well as the software that implements the business rules involved in the circulation of materials to library patrons and the policies that apply for such conditions as length of checkout term, renewals allowed, and fines.

Discovery interfaces likewise offer their own set of personalized patron services, but they are different from those of the ILS. For the discovery product to succeed as a unified interface, it needs to provide a seamless interface involving patron services related to its own features as well as to those of the underlying ILS.

One of the more difficult aspects of implementing a discovery interface separate from the online catalog module of the ILS concerns these patron services. It's important to make the interactions between the ILS and the discovery interface as smooth as possible from the perspective of the end users. Having the user log in to the discovery interface and the online catalog of the ILS as separate operations would not, for example, be a very friendly approach. It's better to allow the users to sign in to the discovery interface and then gracefully pass the user into the local ILS service request pages.

The techniques for presenting real-time information about the status of an item vary across the discovery systems. One of the common approaches relies on deep linking into the Web-based interface of the ILS for the presentation of the detailed view of an item and for access to relevant patron services. With this method, the discovery interface uses a persistent URL to invoke a page that is delivered by the ILS. It requires that the ILS includes the ability to address any resource that it manages through a predictable and persistent URL. The page presented through this URL may be a generic display as seen through the native online catalog, or it may be a page designed specifically for the discovery interface.

Another method of interaction between the ILS and the discovery interface relies more on behind-the-scenes communications to allow the discovery interface to manage the presentation of all pages seen by the end user. This approach takes advantage of industry standard protocols or other applications programming interfaces (APIs) that support the transfer of data from the ILS to the discovery interface regarding the current location and availability of the item. The presentation of a reasonably complete set of patron services requires an even fuller set of API functions that support services involving patron interactions.

▶ EXTRACT DATA FROM THE ILS

One of the first steps of implementing a discovery interface involves extracting data from the ILS. The basic descriptive metadata regarding this aspect of the library's collection almost always takes the form of MARC21 records, an international standard implemented in all major ILS products. The basic MARC record does not provide all of the information needed by the discovery interface. The extraction process will also require data regarding holding locations, copies, and other item-specific information beyond the basic MARC record. Some discovery systems will benefit from the extraction of the authority files managed within the ILS.

The onus of the data extraction work usually resides in the library, especially if the discovery product comes from a source other than the ILS. This task will tap the resources of those who manage the ILS. In most cases the library will have a systems librarian, automation specialist, or other personnel with expertise in the internal workings of the ILS. Some libraries have more outsourced arrangements for the maintenance of their automation system. In either case, some discovery interface providers will not have the ability to perform the extraction of data from your ILS. They may, however, have previous experience with other libraries using your ILS and will have detailed instructions to guide you in getting data out in the form needed.

For this phase of the implementation project, it's often possible to obtain advice and assistance from peer institutions. The implementation of discovery interfaces separate from the ILS has become relatively commonplace. In most cases you should be able to identify other libraries using your ILS that have also implemented the discovery interface you selected. The body of expertise surrounding the process of operating discovery interfaces with ILS products continues to expand. Libraries usually are willing to share information and experience with colleagues. Libraries can exploit a number of sources to identify others with applicable experience. In addition to mailing lists related to either the discovery product or the ILS, the discovery interface vendor may have developed documentation for each major ILS and will have lists of reference sites. You can also use the advanced search feature of the lib-web-cats directory in Library Technology Guides to identify libraries using your ILS that have also implemented your discovery interface (see www.libarytechnology .org).

The process of extracting data out of the ILS should not differ greatly among the specific discovery products. Procedures developed by another library using your ILS for data extraction may be helpful even if used with another discovery product. The ability to extract data from the library's automation system is an important capability that may be needed for other kinds of projects such as participation in a union catalog, system migration, and databases clean-up projects or authorities processing.

The data being extracted may come from different places within the ILS. You can expect, for example, to extend each MARC record with 9xx fields that describe each item held by each branch. This technique closely resembles that used when extracting data from one ILS to migrate to another. Current status data may come from an entirely different part of the system than the bibliographic database.

The metadata model of the discovery interfaces in libraries closely follows that established by the Open Archives Initiative Protocol for Metadata Harvesting (www.openarchive.org). OAI-PMH provides a very convenient method for the transfer of metadata from the ILS. Harvesting has become a major method and increasingly displaces federated searching methods that rely on real-time search and retrieval protocols. In earlier phases of library automation, this broadcast search model, typically implemented through the Z39.50 protocols, dominated. Today, it's much more common to create search services based on harvesting complete sets of metadata. OAI-PMH provides a standard for the transfer of data from information repositories to search services. The protocol was created to support services that could provide access to content distributed among many different e-print servers, which were gaining wider use within many academic and research communities. The model of creating a search service based on harvested metadata from multiple repositories has since become the preferred model of federated search.

OAI-PMH involves a very simple set of directives and was designed for flexibility regarding metadata formats. Dublin Core was specified as the default metadata format for OAI-PMH, but MARC and other schemes can be used as well.

OAI-PMH involves equipping information repositories with a responder that listens for requests for metadata and a harvesting agent associated with a service that wants to make use of the metadata. The initial visit of the harvesting agent essentially requests all of the metadata available. The repository will respond to the request, delivering metadata on its own terms. It may, for example, provide a limited amount of metadata, ending with a resumption token that instructs the agent when to return for more. This mechanism helps the repository avoid overload conditions where a harvesting agent might request large amounts of metadata during periods of peak load. The resumption token can be used to shift metadata requests to convenient periods.

Given the similarity of metadata workflows between what was created for the Open Archives Initiative and for library discovery interfaces, OAI-PMH provides a convenient mechanism in this arena. Rather than reinvent the process of extracting metadata from each ILS or other repository, it may be possible to take advantage of existing programming that implements OAI-PMH.

Even when using OAI-PMH for the extraction of metadata from the ILS into the discovery interface, it will be necessary to do some formatting of the harvested records. It will probably be necessary, for example, to configure the OAI-PMH responder to deliver MARC records bundled with holdings and item-level data.

The OAI-PMH approach can be especially helpful when multiple repositories populate the discovery interface. In a consortium, for example, a discovery interface may need to interact with the ILS in several different libraries. Content from other repositories may also be brought into the discovery interface through OAI-PMH. Digital repository products such as CONTENTdm, DSpace, and Fedora come with OAI-PMH support built in.

▶ IMPORT DATA INTO THE DISCOVERY INTERFACE

Once the data have been extracted from the ILS, they are loaded into the discovery interface. Again, each product has its own requirements, but some general patterns apply.

The search engines of the discovery interfaces will interact with the data much differently than the ILS did. Especially for the MARC data extracted from the ILS, there may be opportunities to expand and enrich the data to better take advantage of the capabilities of the search engine of the discovery interface. These are some other opportunities for enriching MARC data for improved retrieval:

▶ Matching and loading tables of contents, summaries, and reviews from sources such as Syndetic Solutions, Syndetics ICE, Baker and Taylor Content Café, Google Book Search, and Amazon Web Services

▶ Using data from the authority file to provide enhanced retrieval by variants of names or related subject headings

▶ Obtaining full texts of items when available

The MARC data extracted out of the ILS will be processed in various ways as it loads into the discovery interface.

One of the challenges at hand involves shaping the way that the metadata from the ILS and other data sources will be used within the discovery interface:

▶ How will MARC tags be weighted in the search engine when determining relevancy?
▶ What facet categories will be implemented, and what fields will be used to populate them?
▶ What fields will display on the result lists and full record displays, and how will they be labeled?

The answers to these questions will depend on the implementation and customization procedures of the discovery interface involved. Even though the procedures differ among products, it's essential to analyze and assess the incoming metadata and how they impact each element of the discovery interface and bear on search features, especially relevancy ranking.

Each discovery interface product will have its own set of implementation procedures. In most cases there should be a default configuration that provides a reasonable set of options for the way that records index and display. The extent to which the library may customize or tune these options varies. The key challenge involves gaining a good understanding of how the data extracted from the ILS and other repositories are represented within the discovery interface and understanding the procedures for tuning and configuring the system to provide the best results for your library's users.

The discovery interface may also be able to take advantage of the authority records managed within the ILS to provide consistency of names and subject headings and to produce cross references in the online catalog. It may, for example, use authority data to enhance searching, but it will probably use different mechanisms than found in traditional online catalogs. Blending bibliographic and authority data makes it possible to automatically include items that match related terms in the search results.

A major initiative helped to standardize the process of connecting ILSs with discovery interfaces. The Digital Library Federation charged a group called the Integrated Library System Discovery Interface (ILS-DI) Task Group to investigate opportunities for interoperability. The group developed a proposal for an API that addressed the core areas of intersection between these two types of systems. The recommendations of the ILS-DI group were presented to a group of developers of discovery systems and ILS vendors in a pair of meetings at the University of California at Berkeley in March 2008 and August 2008, resulting in a set of key functions known as the Berkeley Accords. The work of the ILS-DI group provides an API that addresses the complex interactions between these two categories of software. This API provides a pragmatic framework for interoperability but has not become a universally adopted standard.

The discussions of this meeting identified three areas essential for a basic programmatic interface between an ILS and discovery systems. These functions are harvesting, availability, and linking. Harvesting involves the wholesale and incremental export of records from the ILS. OAI-PMH addresses this functionality and was proposed as the preferred binding for this function. Availability involves providing a mechanism for a discovery interface to determine the real-time circulation status of an item known to the discovery interface through a harvested record. The proposed binding for availability would be a simple REST interface that returns item status data. Linking provides a stable mechanism for invoking a page for a given item that provides detailed information and any relevant services, such as placing a hold or recall.

This led to the focus on these three functions (harvesting, availability, and linking), with many of the details to be worked out in the future. All of the developer representatives were polled about their commitment toward supporting these recommendations. Most voted to support the recommendations, though many stipulated qualifications depending on how the details were resolved in the future. Innovative Interfaces abstained with the same basic concern. The general consensus surrounding these functions as the basis for the ILS Basic Discovery Interface has also been called the Berkeley Accord.

For more information on the history of the integration of traditional ILSs and the new discovery interface, see Breeding, Marshall. 2008. "Progress on the DLS ILS Discovery Interface API: The Berkeley Accord." *Information Standards Quarterly* (Summer): 18–19.

▶ ESTABLISH REAL-TIME INTERACTIONS

It's essential for the discovery system to interact with the ILS in real time in order to accurately reflect the status of materials and to provide relevant services. Remember that the ILS continues to be the application that acquires, describes, and circulates library materials. The discovery system periodically harvests data en masse from the ILS, but it also needs to perform some actions in real time against live data.

Most information retrieval systems, including this genre of discovery systems, respond to a query with a listing of results presented in a relatively brief format. When the user selects any given record, the full information for that item displays. The brief format may be limited to what can fit within one or two lines. The full display devotes an entire page to the item, often divided into sections selected through tab headings.

Because discovery systems work on the basis of information harvested from the ILS, they will almost always have enough information readily available for the initial brief display. These brief listings must convey enough information to help identify items of interest, inviting the user to click through to see more details.

I noted earlier that discovery interfaces follow one of two different techniques for the display of a full record: deep linking through a persistent, resource-specific URL to hand off the display to the underlying ILS; or dynamically within the discovery interface using a combination of harvested data and information retrieved in real time through a background request to the ILS using an API.

The implementation tasks involved with the real-time interactions depend on the technique your discovery system uses. For those that depend on deep linking to pages generated by the ILS, the library will need to work with the ILS vendor to ensure a viable persistent URL that can be used to link to any given resource. The look and feel of the discovery interface will likely differ from that of the native online catalog. The library will want to customize the page presented by the ILS to blend with the discovery interface. Most ILS products provide tools to control the look and layout of such pages, using templates, cascading style sheets, or other configuration utility.

The support of patron-specific services requires attention to how the interface will deal with authentication relative to other systems used in the library. Ideally patrons should only need to sign in once to gain access to the various services and resources offered throughout the library's Web environment. Discovery systems usually offer their own personalized services feature that requires a patron to sign in. This account may allow the user to save resources, reuse queries, set up alerts, set up a profile of preferred resources, and the like. Other applications in the library environment may also have their own personalized services that require patrons to sign in, such as the following:

- ▶ The ILS for renewals, holds, and other requests
- ▶ A proxy server for access to licensed electronic resources
- ▶ Interlibrary loan request systems

In a campus or corporate environment, it's also highly desired to use the same authentication credentials used for other institutional resources such as e-mail, calendaring, file storage, and the like.

Complex environments will often include an authentication service that manages the log-in process for each application used by the organization. This authentication service allows a person to use a single username and password, digital certificate, or other secure credential for access to multiple services. Multiple protocols and components exist for providing authentication services, including LDAP (lightweight directory access protocol), Microsoft Windows Active Directory, Kerberos, and CAS (Central Authentication Service). Some library automation vendors have developed their own authentication components, such as PDS (Patron Directory Services) from Ex Libris, the Patron API from Innovative Interfaces, and Remote Patron Authentication from SirsiDynix. Each of these products either manages the authentication of library services through an external authentication service or allows the patron database of the ILS to operate as an authentication service.

In libraries with a more complex infrastructure involving multiple applications, one of the major implementation tasks for the discovery interface involves configuring it to operate smoothly with an authentication authorization environment, resulting in a single sign-on capability for library uses as they interact with the discovery interfaces, the content delivered through each associated system or repository, and the patron services associated with each type of content.

▶ PROVIDE FOR ONGOING SYNCHRONIZATION

Because the data managed within the ILS changes continually, the discovery interface would quickly become out of date without some means for continual updates. The synchronization of the discovery interface with the ILS resembles that of the initial extraction and load process but is limited to changes made since the last update. The scripts or ILS reports used for the initial data transfer can be used with the same options and scheduled to run at a regular interval.

The frequency of updating will depend on a number of library-specific factors. The discovery platform should be kept into the closest synchronization with the ILS as is reasonably practical. Items added or modified will not appear in the discovery system until the next iteration of the update script. Libraries that process higher numbers of new materials may be motivated to update very frequently. Some discovery systems rely completely on real-time interactions for circulation status, while others present the status of items based on harvested data, providing the real-time status only when the user selects an item. Discovery systems that depend on harvested information to show the circulation status in results listings benefit from very frequent updates. The time that it takes for the update script to process may also impact the frequency. Taking all these factors into consideration, the frequency of updating may range from several times per hour to once or twice per day. The same considerations apply to other repositories besides the ILS that populate the discovery interface.

▶ LOAD CONTENT FROM OTHER REPOSITORIES

We've noted the value of populating discovery environments to interact with all the different components of a library's collection. While the ILS may represent the most complex system for data transfer and user interactions, bringing in the content from other information resources will follow a similar, possibly simplified, model. The basic workflow of data extraction from the original repository, configuring indexing and display features, providing mechanisms for proper authentication and authorization, and presenting content items apply.

When populating the discovery interface with repositories other than the ILS, many of the issues that need to be addressed surround metadata. Non-ILS repositories will likely work with XML, and with metadata standards such as Dublin Core. Populating the discovery interface from these repositories will involve the same cycle of workflow, beginning with the initial comprehensive extraction of data, incremental transfers of new and changed records for synchronization, and mechanisms for linking users to content items.

Tasks that apply to the integration of content from these repositories will include the configuration details regarding how the discovery interface will handle each field for indexing and display. As the metadata or full-text content from additional repositories needs to be proportionately represented in search results, the intermingling of MARC, Dublin Core, article citation metadata, and full text presents an enormous challenge in discovery interfaces to deliver balanced search results where none of the repositories represented overwhelms the others and each appears appropriately in the search results.

Chapter 2 noted some emerging discovery products that include large-scale prepopulated indexes representing large collections of e-journals, citation databases, and even WorldCat.org. As described, products such as Summon will also harvest the metadata from the local ILS and blend them into the library's view of the index. We can anticipate a similar set of procedures for extracting data from the ILS and dealing with real-time status display and patron services as seen with the earlier discovery products, as well as a need to ensure that search results proportionally represent collection components.

▶ BE AWARE OF CATALOGING AND METADATA ISSUES

Metadata play a vital role in a new generation discovery interface. Traditional catalogs have been around a long time, and there is a great deal of experience in the way that they use the nuances of MARC records. These new discovery interfaces exercise metadata in much different ways than the traditional online catalogs. The new products rely on metadata, whether in MARC or some other form, to create facets, as factors in relevancy ranking, and in many other ways not exploited in traditional catalogs. Many of these new interfaces attempt to make even more advanced use of metadata than traditional catalogs especially in the ways that they group and organize records. Concepts such as the Functional Requirements for Bibliographic Records (FRBR) have taken hold in discovery interfaces far beyond what was possible to accomplish in traditional online catalogs.

To the extent that these new interfaces approach metadata differently, there may be large implications for cataloging and authority control within the ILS and in the treatment of metadata in other repositories ingested into the discovery interface. Once exposed in this new way, inconsistencies in metadata become conspicuous that were previously hidden. Especially in the generation of facets, any errors and inconsistencies stand out in full view that took a careful eye to discover in the online catalog.

If the discovery interface combines collections that were previously isolated from each other, a number of metadata issues may arise. If the approach involves merging duplicate bibliographic entries, careful attention will need to be given to such things as match criteria and record inconsistencies.

To the extent that the new discovery environment combines resources that were previously separate, the library will need to enforce consistent metadata practices across its collections to the largest extent possible. Experienced metadata specialists will be important assets in this environment of new discovery methods.

These examples illustrate that the implementation of a new discovery interface may require a great deal of attention to cataloging and metadata issues. A great deal of metadata cleanup may be necessary to optimize the functionality of the new interface. While it seems counterintuitive, these new environments that involve less structured search techniques for users benefit from precise metadata and rigorous cataloging practices.

▶ INTEGRATE ARTICLE-LEVEL CONTENT

We've emphasized that the vision shared by most of the discovery interfaces involves providing access to all components of the library's collection, including the individual articles available through library subscriptions. Libraries allocate large portions of their collection budgets to e-journals and will benefit from more powerful tools for providing access to users. Traditional online catalogs generally describe journal titles and the issues held rather than provide full metadata to the individual articles contained within.

There are two techniques to include the content of individual articles in the search box of the discovery interface. Direct indexing places articles within the native index of the discovery product, and federated searching draws in article content through dynamically querying the servers of the subscription providers.

Direct Indexing

Ideally, the metadata representing the citations, or even the full text, of the articles represented within the library's subscriptions can be indexed directly by the discovery interface. This technique allows the content to be part of the unified search experience, replete with the expected search features of relevancy ranking and faceted navigation.

While it's theoretically possible for a library to gain access to this article level content and to incorporate it into the indexes that they maintain locally, the difficulty of negotiating for access to the content from a wide array of providers and the technical work of indexing these large bodies of material and ongoing additions are daunting.

Some libraries may already have access to collections of articles. In this case, the material can be harvested and indexed following much the same models described for the ILS and other repositories. The quantity and quality of the metadata will require a great deal of attention to ensure balanced representation as it is searched alongside other material. Any library that engages in local indexing of article-level collections will need to be prepared to invest significant resources, in terms of both computing capacity and technical personnel, to this activity.

Some discovery services have recently begun to provide large collections of article content already incorporated into their indexes. This saves libraries from the large burden of gathering and indexing article-level content and the technical infrastructure involved.

Even though such a service avoids the enormity of local indexing, some implementation tasks will apply. A detailed profiling of the library's collection of e-journals will be needed to ensure that the scope of what's searched through the discovery interface aligns with current holdings. This profiling is also needed so that the links provided to the articles from the discovery system connect to the appropriate version that corresponds to the library's subscriptions. Keep in mind that the discovery system only provides indexing for the purpose of discovery and that the presentation of the articles themselves takes place through the servers of the providers.

Federated Searching

The new discovery interfaces tend not to favor federated searching as their primary means to access to the multiple resources that comprise library collections. Several of the products do employ integrated federated search applications in order to bring in resources that cannot be brought in through the preferred harvesting techniques. Even when the library uses a discovery product equipped with a prepopulated index of e-journal content, it will likely require access to specialized resources not covered. To provide access to these specialized resources through the same interface, an integrated federated search component is a pragmatic solution, though less powerful than direct indexing.

From the perspective of implementation, various configuration and integration tasks will need to be addressed. Targets will need to be selected and configured. Common configurations for federated search applications involve grouping targets according to discipline in order to minimize the number of simultaneous sessions maintained and to return more focused results. When integrated with a discovery interface, similar concepts apply, complicated by the need to provide ways for the user to select between the results delivered through federated search and those returned through the products' native indexes.

The control of the way that a discovery interface integrates with a federated search application may be limited. Which federated search applications are supported and how they are configured and customized will usually be specified as part of the installation of the discovery interface. If a library already has a federated search application in place, it may be possible to carry forward at least some of the configuration provided that the discovery interface supports the specific product involved.

Link Resolvers

Most libraries with large collections of e-journal content use a link resolver to provide dynamic linking based on a profile of the library's subscriptions. Link resolvers rely on identifiers or metadata provided by the search context to calculate the valid URL for an article or journal title. To the extent that the discovery interface covers e-journal content, the library will need to verify that the link resolver functions correctly within this context. The knowledge base and subscription profiles that underlie the link resolver must be in synch with that of the discovery interface. If the link resolver and the discovery interface come from the same provider, the knowledge base and subscription profiles may be identical, greatly simplifying this concern. A common scenario involves the discovery interface, link resolver, and federated search components packaged together.

▶ INCLUDE ENRICHED CONTENT

In Chapter 2, I noted that one of the expectations of the new generation of interfaces includes much more attention to visual design and appeal than was commonly seen in legacy online catalogs. The display of cover art within the interface has become a standard feature. One of the implementation tasks will be to choose where to obtain these images and attend to the technical details of incorporating them. In addition to images, the basic bibliographic content can be enriched through additional textual information such as the table of contents, summaries, author biographies, and reviews.

Cover art and other content components can be obtained from a variety of sources, some free and others requiring a paid subscription. Some discover interfaces come with support for a variety of content enrichment options, and the main configuration task simply involves making a selection through its management utility. It's common for discovery products to offer both subscription-based and free enrichment options. Once selected, the discovery interface manages the details of pulling in the enrichment elements. The library might have some control over the page layout, placement, and presentation style.

Some discovery products allow the library to directly manage the technical details involved with enriched content. Libraries that opt to do their own integration of content enrichment elements will need to become familiar with the API offered by the provider and will need to have some access and control over the part of the discovery interface that involves page display. The technical tasks will include programmatically generating a request to the provider based on the ISBN or other unique identifier associated with the item. This request may be as simple as dynamically building a URL following the prescribed formula, or it may require more complex programming. The more technical approach applies primarily to open source discovery interfaces. The commercially produced products handle this feature through configuration options and do not require the library to manage the technical details.

▶ PLAN THE PRACTICAL ASPECTS OF IMPLEMENTATION

Implementing a new discovery interface is a multifaceted project that requires a great deal of planning and coordination. We've identified the major tasks that need to be accomplished in the course of implementation and what's involved in ongoing maintenance. The type of product chosen will determine the scale of each of these tasks. For vendor-hosted "software as a service" options, a given task may be as simple as selecting a feature as part of the subscription agreement. Locally installed versions tend to require more library involvement to technical details. Projects based on open source software will naturally involve more technical and functional complexity.

Project Management

As part of its general administrative environment, a library should already have well-established procedures and infrastructure for managing projects. I don't presume to prescribe any given methodology for project management but do advise libraries to engage in the process.

Each of the tasks mentioned in this chapter will have a different scope, duration, and allocation of effort depending on the type of product involved; the size and complexity of the library; and the quantity and diversity of resources to be delivered through the discovery interface. The project timeline will step through the phases of planning, procurement, and implementation. While the stakeholders for each phase will likely remain fairly constant, the individuals performing the work will vary.

Deployment

One of the important considerations in the implementation of a new discovery interface involves the way that it is deployed to library personnel and to patrons. Few libraries would make an instantaneous switch into a new environment without some kind of preliminary vetting. Depending on local considerations, a variety of strategies could be followed in rolling out a new discovery interface.

Internal Testing

At some point very early in the implementation process, the discovery interface comes to life. In the earliest stages it may not include the desired customizations and all the content elements, and it may not yet perform correctly or adequately. While the staff working through the implementation will understand that it's a work in progress, presenting the system at this early stage to a wider audience could be counterproductive. Exposing the discovery interface at this early stage without managing expectations through proper caveats will not instill confidence in the final product. During this phase of early installation and configuration, many libraries choose not to provide access to a wide group of library personnel or to patrons. During this internal testing phase, a key activity will be aggressively testing every search and display feature to ensure that it meets the requirements in the project specifications or procurement documents.

Staff Preview

Once the discovery interface reaches a certain threshold of completeness and stability, you can begin to expand the user audience. Prior to this preview phase, the functionality of the basic features should be verified and any remaining problems documented. A library may choose to begin a preview of the system before all minor problems have been solved; users included in the preview should be advised of known issues.

Libraries may opt for a variety of ways to offer a preview of a new discover service. An early layer of the preview might be open only to library personnel, possibly limited through IP address restrictions or by their username and password. Even though discovery interfaces target end users, providing early access to library staff enables a wider group to become involved in testing and critical analysis. Giving library personnel access at the earliest stage in which the software is properly functional should also help ensure that staff not feel excluded from the process and give them time to start building expertise with the system that will be essential once it's available to users.

The staff preview will likely uncover a variety of errors and issues that need attention. Obvious problems should be corrected, and this will reinforce with the staff that their time is well spent. Problems that persist for too long once identified may erode confidence in the product or in the implementation process. Some problems may take longer to resolve. Documenting known problems will ensure that staff members know that what they have reported has been duly registered and will save time in having to repeatedly explain the same problems.

It's also during this phase that issues may arise involving the differences in expectations between how library personnel approach search and retrieval and the discovery techniques designed for library users. Don't be surprised when a library staff member reports as a problem a feature that works as designed. These reports provide opportunities to further develop the conversations among library personnel regarding the fundamental differences between discovery interfaces and traditional catalogs.

Public Preview

The next level of preview may involve library users. During this phase, the legacy online catalog remains in place but may have a link inviting users to try their search with the library's new interface. At this stage, the interface should be nearing final form, with all of the major problems identified during the staff preview resolved.

A public preview may have a variety of goals and provides many different kinds of opportunities for feedback from the product's intended audience. It's important to implant a convenient mechanism for users to make comments and report problems. While only a small fraction of those who use the interface will contribute comments, even if they experience difficulties, every fragment of information regarding user reaction to the new interface will be helpful in identifying problems and gauging satisfaction.

The public preview provides an opportunity for library users to gain some exposure prior to it becoming established as the primary, or possibly, sole interface. Those used to the legacy catalog can continue to perform their research without having to figure out something new. The availability of the traditional catalog and other search tools will be especially important if the new discovery interface has not yet been populated with the full span of collection components.

The frequency with which users choose the new discovery interface during this public preview can be an indicator of acceptance. If possible, try to measure whether patrons repeatedly come back to the new discovery interface once they have tried it out instead of using the traditional catalog. These usage patterns can be important indicators. In Chapter 6 we will look at some of the tools for measuring and analyzing usage patterns.

Alternative Interface

The library may instead choose to offer both the traditional catalog and the new discovery interface as more or less equally positioned alternatives. At this point, the interface should be in final form, fully populated, and able to function as a complete alternative to the legacy online catalog.

Offering a transition period during which both the traditional online catalog and the discovery interface are available has both advantages and disadvantages. It is good for those used to the traditional catalog to be able to try the new interface at their leisure. On the down side, offering dual options adds complexity. Users may not understand why they should choose one over the other and may gravitate to one of the options based on its position on the library's Web page or by what they recognize as familiar. This approach also comes with the need for the library to maintain both environments.

Default Interface

The final phase of implementation comes when the new discovery interface takes its place as the default search tool on the library's Web site. While this point marks the end of a long process of implementation, it isn't necessarily the time to sit back and relax. Rather, it's a point where the library should heighten its attention. No matter how much the library attempts to preview and promote the new interface, it will not receive a critical mass of use until it's positioned as the default means of accessing the library's collection. A library does not really know how the majority of its users will react to the new interface until it reaches this stage. This transition warrants careful attention to the metrics indicating use levels, any rise in reports of problems, and careful monitoring of the technical environment to ensure that it performs well under full load.

Switching the new interface in as the default interface should not be done without retaining the option and flexibility to back off. While disrupting the transition would not be ideal, problems may present themselves that may need some time to resolve. Going back to the status quo may be the best means to gain that time.

In academic libraries, it's almost traditional to implement new services during a period when classes are still in session with the goal of having them ready by the beginning of a new term. This strategy may not be ideal for this kind of product. Libraries might consider switching the default interface during the beginning of the break so that all use during this slower period takes place through the new interface. This strategy provides a gentler break-in period and more flexibility for roll-back than the traditional cycle of launching a new service just in time for the new academic year.

▶ MONITOR AND MAINTAIN THE SYSTEM

Once the project reaches completion, activity continues, but on a lower level. All of the environments that require a harvesting and synchronization of content from the ILS and other local repositories will need ongoing monitoring and maintenance. Many libraries will want to expand the content resources addressed by the discovery interface beyond the set included in the initial implementation. As libraries develop new resources through digitization projects and other activities, they will likely want these to be covered by the discovery interface. Periodically new versions of the software or service will need to be tested and rolled into production as well.

Maintenance of the discovery interface will need to be integrated into the routine operations of the library. Ongoing issues will need to be addressed through some aspect of library governance, whether through a standing committee or through assigning responsibility to one or more library personnel. The same types of administrative, functional, and technical tasks performed during implementation will occur during ongoing maintenance as well. The success of the discovery interface will depend on allocating adequate resources to ensure that it operates correctly and evolves in step with changes in the library's collections and services.

Finally, the library will want to measure the impact of its new discovery service. In Chapter 6 we will discuss various aspects of collecting and analyzing usage data, not just about the discovery interface itself but also about the broader set of resources to which it provides access. By analyzing usage data, the library can assess the effectiveness of the product and fine tune its performance and make improvements in the way that it delivers access to library collections.

▶ KEEP ABREAST OF EMERGING TRENDS

We've been looking at discovery interfaces, dissecting their features, scanning current products, and working through issues of implementation. By no means have we seen the end of movement within this genre of products and related technologies. In this section I review how the genre has played out so far and consider some of the possibilities as it moves into the future.

The idea of discovery interfaces separate from the online catalogs delivered with ILSs isn't especially recent. I noted that as early as 2000 Medialab Solutions had begun offering AquaBrowser as a replacement to the traditional model of library catalog. But the real competition began in 2006 when Encore and Primo joined the fray.

Progressive Evolution of the Genre

We've seen a progressive evolution in the field of discovery interfaces, with a bar set ever higher on features and functionality. In the early phase of the product genre, features such as relevancy ranking of results, faceted navigation, and use of cover art were novel improvements over the staid legacy online catalogs. The model of separating discovery from the ILS and other automation component has become well accepted. Today these features and concepts fall within the expected minimal feature set of a discovery system. No product would be well accepted without them.

Once the product genre had become established with a certain set of minimal expectations, new entrants into the field have to work harder to deliver a product concept that stands above the crowd. Not only must new products match the features found in the existing offerings and deliver distinctive capabilities on top, each new version of the existing products must likewise catch up with the newly established norms for features and top them. From the developer's perspective this adds pressure to continually innovate. Libraries benefit from this arms race, and we're seeing products progress at a faster pace than has previously been the norm in the field of library automation.

A Growing Number of Players and Products

The landscape is also becoming ever more crowded. As legacy online catalogs become ever less viable, the opportunities in this arena become vast. While the libraries that have already invested in a next-generation discovery interface number in the hundreds, many thousands remain in the market pool. In an age of diminishing opportunities for sales of new ILSs, discovery systems stand as a great opportunity for those involved in creating library automation software. In Chapter 2 I noted that almost all of the vendors involved in creating ILSs have also launched discovery products or have reengineered their online catalogs to absorb a significant portion of the feature set. Vendors not involved in ILS development, such as Serials Solutions and EBSCO, have tossed their hat in the ring. To further expand the options, libraries themselves have become involved, with products such as VuFind and Blacklight showing promise and the eXtensible Catalog offering a new conceptual approach.

Shared Concepts

In the present state of discovery interfaces some of the foundational concepts have solidified and the basic features have stabilized, and the products and technologies are beginning to mature. One of the solid concepts seen across the products involves discovery as a separate activity from library automation and spanning a broader range of content. All embrace the idea of a centralized index populated as extensively as possible rather than rely on federated search. Relevancy ranking is a given.

Differentiation and Distinction

With these concepts and features established as the norm, it's interesting to see what distinctive qualities each new product entry embraced. The LS2 PAC launched by The Library Corporation emphasized visual design that set a new standard in this area. VuFind offers the basic functionality set with a distinguishing quality of an open source software license, which finds a receptive audience these days. SirsiDynix Enterprise falls mostly within the expected bar of functionality and offers a search engine based on fuzzy matching as its distinguishing quality. VTLS positions its VISUALIZER interface as distinctive through its ability to support FRBR. BiblioCommons makes its splash in the discovery arena through its design around social networking concepts.

Until just recently the competition has focused primarily on the features and functionality of the interface itself and on the technical capabilities of its search engine. Now the competition is shifting to the content addressed by the interface. It's no longer any big deal to offer a product that searches the contents of the ILS with a relevancy ranking and faceted navigation. Pulling in digital collections and other repositories created by the library into the interface is becoming commonplace. Especially for academic libraries with large collections of e-journals, providing access to the articles represented in this aspect of the library collection is paramount. Federated search, even when integrated into the next-gen interface, has not proven entirely satisfactory.

The current phase of one-upmanship focuses on ways to provide access to broad swaths of library collections through prepopulated indexes. The concept of Web-scale discovery describes the ability to search across the complete body of material within a domain. Google exemplifies Web-scale discovery at the broadest level, harvesting and providing access to almost all Web sites that exist and most of the individual resources within each. OCLC's WorldCat can be thought of as approaching Web scale in its ability to search an index that represents a significant portion of the world's books, and it is ever more rapidly growing to meet this goal. Web-scale discovery describes the intent to be comprehensive. In reality the goal may not necessarily be possible, but it seems reasonable to apply the term to a product or service that approaches that ideal with a technology infrastructure capable of scaling to that level. A discovery product that focuses on harvesting and indexing the resources from the ILS and repositories housed by a library might be considered operating on the scale of local resources.

Aiming for Web-Scale Discovery

We currently see a movement to not only meet and exceed the current expectations of the features and functionality of the interface but also to deliver products capable of Web-scale discovery spanning the entire domain of content represented in library collections. OCLC positions itself as Web scale. WorldCat Local gives its users the ability to search the vast WorldCat.org database, primarily books, and has recently begun layering in vast amounts of article metadata through partnerships with companies such as EBSCO. OCLC's strategy involves enhancing its current Web-scale approach to books, to something that approaches Web-scale in addressing e-journal articles and other e-content.

The EBSCO Discovery Service claims similar ambitions, with Web-scale book discovery accomplished through its access to the complete set of WorldCat.org records and the body of article material it plans to assemble with its own resources supplemented by content it plans to fold in from other publishers and partners.

Serials Solutions exhibits the trend toward Web-scale discovery for article content in its Summon product launched in June 2009 and in production use in a growing number of libraries. The product includes an index that represents all the electronic content represented in library collections. At the time of product launch, Serials Solutions reported that its prepopulated index included over 500 million articles. The Web-scale discovery of e-content in Summon is complemented by the indexing on a local scale of the library's holdings from its ILS and other local repositories.

The largest barrier to providing Web-scale discovery of article content has been the reluctance of the providers and publishers of these resources to make them available for indexing. Even though the intent of the indexing is to provide a more efficient means to deliver users to their content, publishers have not been willing to expose their assets wholesale to those interested in indexing the content for discovery systems. Now that precedents have been established, we can anticipate a further liberalizing of access so that true Web-scale discovery of article content can become more of a reality.

Deep Indexing

The next round of progress in the discovery arena involves deepening the indexing of collections beyond metadata to the full text of the material. Seen in this way, deep indexing greatly expands the discoverability of materials by processing the entire text into the indexes, turning each phrase or word into a potential access point for retrieval. A product or service implementing deep searching would also make use of structured metadata to facilitate the ability to support faceted navigation and to support relevance ranking.

Deep indexing is just beginning to emerge as a capability of library discovery interfaces. Serials Solutions reports that Summon performs indexing on the full text of the majority of the articles addressed, combining Web-scale discovery with deep indexing. WorldCat Local, while Web scale in scope, does not perform deep indexing, at least not yet.

The ambition for deep indexing applies to books as well as articles. It's well within sight that all of the books in the world will be digitized. All books today are published using all digital streams and vast quantities of older books have been digitized already, with rapid progress on those remaining. We can anticipate that the next front in discovery will involve taking advantage of this vast body of digitized books to create tools capable of Web-scale and deep indexing to take the discoverability of books to the next level.

Library collections contain many nontextual formats. We can also expect future generations of discovery products to find better ways to handle images, audio, and video. We can imagine going beyond metadata descriptions of these kinds of digital objects to include deep indexing based on transcripts of audio, visual pattern matching, and other retrieval techniques.

Web-scale discovery paired with deep indexing describes an incredibly ambitious strategy for the next wave of discovery products. If possible to accomplish, products with these capabilities open up tremendous opportunities for researchers. It's exciting to imagine a discovery environment encompassing the full breadth of content represented within library collections with each object fully indexed.

Next-Gen Library Automation

At the same time that the realm of discovery interfaces is experiencing rapid progression, we're also seeing the beginnings of some major changes on other fronts in library automation. One of the main themes in this book is the separation of discovery from library automation functions. We saw great urgency in producing better interfaces for library users. The separation of the interfaces used by library patrons from those used by library personnel provided an expedient way to deal with the priorities at hand.

This separation needed to happen because the ILS products available today focus on a narrow scope of content, largely surrounding the physical inventory of the library. Other tools have been adopted for the management of electronic resources and for creating repositories of nonbook content.

We've talked about the ILS and its connections to discovery interfaces. One of the key issues driving the need for discovery interfaces springs from the myopic focus of the ILS on print materials and inadequate attention to electronic content. We've seen a proliferation of applications that have emerged to help libraries deal with electronic content, including link resolvers and electronic resource management systems. The bifurcation of library automation into products that specialize in electronic or print content not only presents difficulties for discovery interfaces but it also leads to inefficiencies in the operations of the library.

An important trend brewing involves efforts to rework the basic automation products used by library personnel behind the scenes. The same shifts in assumptions that drove the need for new interfaces for patrons also demand a new way of looking at the tools that support the work of staff.

The viability of separate and unconnected applications to manage the library collection based on type of material has begun to come into question. A different vision of library automation might involve an automation framework that manages resources agnostic of format type. As a significant proportion of content shifts toward electronic, having an automation system that specializes in print becomes increasingly untenable.

The new generation of library interfaces will be hampered unless the backend software also undergoes changes. The separation of print and electronic resources in the backend library automation systems can be superficially masked through the discovery layer interfaces, but it will eventually be necessary to find ways to manage resources in a more unified way internally in order to provide better methods of discovery and access.

Several projects are now underway that aim to reshape the basic library automation environment. The author has been involved in the Open Library Environment (OLE) Project, which aims to produce a community source library automation format that takes a format-neutral approach to resource management based on the service-oriented architecture. With funding provide by the Andrew W. Mellon Foundation, OLE has engaged in a series of business process modeling exercises conducted at regional workshops to identify the workflows that apply within libraries without the constraints of legacy software. The OLE Project is currently finishing its design phase and preparing for a second phase that will build an open source reference implementation of that design.

Ex Libris has announced that it is working on Universal Resource Management, a new product that will address both electronic and print content. URM will eventually replace both of its traditional ILS products, Aleph and Voyager, as well as its Verde and Meridian electronic resource management systems. URM will embrace the service-oriented architecture and offer a rich set of open APIs that will offer libraries greater flexibility in the way that they use the system.

In yet another approach to reinventing library automation, OCLC has announced that it will extend WorldCat Local to include functionality that will obviate the need for libraries to operate their own ILS and ERM platforms. Based on the concept of cloud computing, OCLC envisions the ability for libraries worldwide to participate in a global Web-based automation environment. We have discussed WorldCat Local as a discovery interface based on the vast WorldCat.org database. Libraries have also routinely used WorldCat for cataloging and interlibrary loan processing. This more recent development involves performing circulation, acquisitions, and license management on the WorldCat Local platform as well. OCLC expects to make this service available to its members in 2010. While the concept of a WorldCat Local cooperative library system isn't without its complications or controversies, it does present a radically new approach to library automation.

In the latest phase of library automation we've seen a number of disruptions from the conventional models that prevailed for many years. We've seen a major revolution in the way that libraries present their collections to their users. The beginnings of change can now be seen in the library automation systems. Both of these movements erupt out of a disconnect between systems that focus too narrowly on physical collections and the reality of complex libraries that deal with digital and physical collections and services.

The players in the industry are in motion. Not that long ago, a group of commercial companies selling proprietary software dominated. Today we see open source making inroads in all aspects of the industry with involvement by both commercial and nonprofit organizations. OCLC, a nonprofit cooperative, has become involved in a big way, expanding its role as a bibliographic utility to one of the major providers of technology to libraries with major involvement across a wide range of products and services, including discovery interfaces and library automation. Largely through open source endeavors, many libraries have taken a much larger role in development in recent years.

Balancing Current Needs with Future Opportunities

Although many changes are still underway, that doesn't necessarily mean that libraries can wait around and see how it all turns out before making any kind of move. Especially when it comes to modernizing the way that libraries offer their collections as services, the strategy of waiting for a final and perfect solution may be counterproductive. There will always be newer and better solutions somewhere on the distant horizon, resulting in a perpetual waiting state. At the time of this writing some of the products have not seen final release. But the cards are basically on the table. And the deck includes a wide range of options in maturity, risk, and cost. Most of all, the options represent a spectrum of conceptual approaches. While libraries must always look forward and try to understand what technologies might be emerging in the future, they must also plan the most expedient course for their present needs.

▶4

MARKETING

We've seen in the preceding chapters the large level of investment behind the launch of a new discovery interface for a library. One of the measures of success of the project will be the level of use and acceptance it receives from its intended audience. In this chapter I explore some of the ways that a library might help increase the use of its discovery product through various marketing techniques.

While it's important to ensure that a new product such as a discovery interface finds adequate levels of use, an even better approach is to think of the new discovery interface as a way to promote the library. The older generation online catalogs haven't done much to enhance the reputation of libraries, at least not recently. In the earlier days of the Web, libraries could have rightly been considered pioneers. We offered some of the very earliest Web-based information resources. As the Web advanced at such a faster pace than the technologies put forward by libraries, our reputation in this area slipped. These new interfaces stand to make up a lot of ground, and, if successful, may help improve the position of libraries as providers of quality information on the Web.

That being said, the task at hand involves ensuring that the new discovery interface is sufficiently promoted, both to the end users it's designed to serve and to library personnel who will find it a part of their daily work lives. In thinking about the marketing of the new discovery interface, some of the goals may include the following:

▶ Prepare library users for an upcoming change in the way that they will gain access to library resources

▶ Educate library users on the benefits of the change

▶ Increase the interest in the new service and in the content it delivers

▶ Prepare and educate library personnel for a new environment that may involve some degree of change for their work activities

▶ Enhance the reputation of the library through association with improved services

Anytime that the library makes a major change in its services, it should take reasonable measures to ensure that its users are well informed in advance. Putting forward advance communications regarding the deployment of the new discovery interface will not only pave the way for the upcoming change in the library's services but also provide opportunities to mention some of the content resources offered by the library. Unfortunately, many library users do not understand the role libraries play in providing access to electronic resources. The publicity related to the new discovery platform will also provide an educational opportunity about the investments that the library makes in content resources.

Consortial implementations bring their own set of challenges to a marketing effort for the new discovery interface. Each consortium has its own way of handling projects and the publicity surrounding them. But in broad strokes, the challenges for communication lie in the distribution of what will be handled by the member libraries and what will take place through the consortium.

▶ ENLIST THE HELP OF PUBLIC RELATIONS EXPERTS

Many libraries have a dedicated capacity for public relations. It's common in municipal libraries, large academic libraries, and others to have a full-time public relations officer. Other libraries delegate public relations responsibility within the portfolio of a senior administrator or charge a committee or workgroup. One of the components of the implementation project should include coordination with the library's public relations unit. Just as the project makes use of technical specialists as needed, the marketing aspects of the projects should be managed by those with that expertise and responsibility. Smaller libraries that do not have personnel dedicated to public relations may be able to enlist assistance from students enrolled in a communications or marketing program or community members with expertise in this area. The project may also provide an opportunity for creative staff members without formal training but with an interest in marketing to become involved.

▶ USE A VARIETY OF MARKETING CHANNELS

In the marketing of this new service, the library can take advantage of a number of channels that may already be in place, as well as consider establishing new channels that may have not been previously established.

External Outlets

Some of the traditional venues that the library might use to publicize its new discovery environment include feature articles in the local and campus newspapers, which may be published either in print or on the Web. Access to these external channels, because they are not under the direct control of the library, will depend on being able to attract the attention of the editors or publishers. Those involved in the marketing of the project will need to determine what media outlets would be most likely to develop and publish a story on the library's new service—local, professional, national.

If the library's discovery interface can be considered to be especially innovative, an early deployment of a product, or delivering some unique capability, it might warrant coverage in the national media of the library profession. This type of recognition isn't so much directed at the clientele of the library but to enhance the reputation of the library in a way that might pave the way for new funding or operational opportunities.

Whether the library wants coverage in local or national publications, it needs to develop a press release and distribute it to the intended outlets. The press release is the standard mechanism for

eliciting coverage through external media. A good press release follows a standard formula with the following elements:

▶ A self-explanatory title
▶ The date and city of the release
▶ A complete synopsis of the accomplishment in the first paragraph
▶ Supporting quotations from high-level officials and key partici-
pants and explanatory text in subsequent paragraphs
▶ Standard verbiage describing each of the participating organiza-
tions
▶ The name and contact data for press inquiries

A successful press release can provide sufficient information for a
brief news-oriented story, but it aims to elicit the interest of a journalist
or editor. The press contact should be prepared with the themes that
the library would like to emphasize in the story in a follow-up press in-
terview and be briefed with sufficient details to respond to questions.
In most cases the press contact should be an administrator or public
relations specialist, not the technical lead. Referrals can be made for
follow-up interviews with project managers or technical staff if
needed.

Most colleges, universities, and municipalities have a public relations office that will provide assistance to the library in publicizing
high-profile projects. Some organizations may have specific policies
that require all press issues to flow through the official public relations
channels and not directly from individual units such as the library.

Internal Marketing Channels

A library has more discretion in the way that it uses its internal resources for the promotion of a new service. Opportunities in this area
include campuswide publications and Web sites and publications and
communications channels that emerge from the library directly.

Consider working with publications that are external to the library
itself but within its parent organization. These can be helpful vehicles
to publicize and promote the project. In an academic setting, these
channels are ideal for reaching the core clientele of faculty and students. Both official university and student-run publications fall into
this category.

For coverage in official university media the library will need to
work directly with its public relations office. Having an ongoing relationship with this office will greatly benefit the library not only for the

internal publicity of its new discovery platform but also for other major initiatives in which the library engages over time. Having a public relations officer from the college or university level involved with the library's marketing efforts brings in expertise and resources beyond what the library may have internally.

The library may be able to work with the campus media department that develops content for the main Web site for the college or university to appear as a featured story or news item. Increasingly campus media offices manage their Web sites as promotional vehicles and actively pursue projects and activities that highlight organizational accomplishments. The development of a powerful interface for providing new ways to access the library's vast collections may fall well within the kinds of activities a university media office would be interested in featuring in its internal Web site and publications.

The next level of marketing involves the publications and media developed and distributed directly by the library. For many public libraries, this may be the primary focus of a marketing effort because they may not have public relations units available through a higher level organization. The marketing plan for the project should exploit any existing publications or other communications channels already in place as well as any that might need to be specifically created.

The library might, for example, want to craft one or more articles on the service to appear in its own publications. Many libraries regularly publish a newsletter, distributed to its clientele and supporters. Developing a feature on the product with follow-up progress reports helps keep the project in the general awareness of its readers. Within the library's own publications, it has the discretion to provide a more in-depth treatment of the capabilities of the discovery interface than is likely possible with external media. While avoiding complex technical details, a feature written for an internal library publication may be the best opportunity to provide a full explanation of the technologies involved, the content covered, and the flavor of the interface employed. This feature could be written in such a way that it could also be incorporated into the library's Web site as a part of the documentation it offers on its collections and services.

A printed brochure is another practical piece of marketing collateral in support of the new discovery platform. While electronic publications may reach a broader audience, it is also helpful to have something that can be available at library service desks, handed out in bibliographic instruction sessions, library tours, and orientation visits, and distributed in campus mailings.

The content of a brochure will be shaped by those involved with the project and familiar with its capabilities and with the anticipated issues and questions that library users might have. In the design of the brochure, consider giving a very basic explanation of the service, illustrative graphics, and some indication of the content covered. Because the specific resources might change over time, any printed material needs to be written in such a way as to not go out of date as the content evolves.

New Media

If a library has a blog, then it should be part of the ramp-up toward the launch of the new service. Blogs lend themselves to an informal, low-profile, but sustained campaign to communicate with uses regarding new services. Because blog posts take a serial flavor, it's possible to provide information about the service through a series of posts, each focusing on a different aspect. This information should also be distributed through RSS feeds or through Twitter to expand distribution to those more engaged with these channels.

Other new media approaches to publicizing the service include creating podcasts and videos. Many libraries already incorporate audio and video media into their general communications and marketing strategies. Those who haven't yet broken out of the realm of text-only communications may find that the launch of a new discovery interface that is itself engaged with multimedia content an ideal opportunity to begin.

▶ MANAGE THE MESSAGE

Libraries have a variety of channels available to publicize and promote their initiatives. In the case of the rollout of a new discovery interface, the library will need to decide the right level of advance publicity. While it's good to provide an adequate level of information in advance, it's not necessarily the one issue that should dominate the channels in which the library communicates with its users.

As the library produces promotional content regarding the new discovery interface, it's important to convey its vision as concisely as possible. As much as the library may be invested in creating the service, library users have a much more fleeting interest and will not necessarily take a great deal of time to read a detailed exposition about the nuances of its benefits and how it works.

The promotion of a specific resource such as a discovery interface is a component of the library's broader marketing strategies. Don't contradict or overwhelm any existing marketing efforts. It might not be desirable, for example, to promote the URL of the discovery interface independently of that of the library. Many libraries prefer to consistently use their main URL in all marketing and other literature. Any given resource as the recipient of special promotion should be conspicuous on the library's Web page.

The Role of Instruction

Positioned as a new tool for providing access to the library's collection, the discovery interface will be an important part of the programs in bibliographic instruction. The new generation of discovery products aims to work more consistently with the way that users experience the Web. If the products live up to that ideal, then the publicity should focus on the broad vision, not on the details of how to operate the interface. From the perspective of bibliographic instruction, the mechanics of how to operate the interface might be less of a focus, leaving more time for content relating to exploring search results and collections components involved.

Bibliographic instruction or information literacy sessions can also be a marketing tool. I noted in Chapter 2 that it's vital to include those involved in instruction at the earliest stage of planning because they often require substantial lead time to adjust the curriculum and develop handouts or other materials. This early involvement can also be leveraged to help promote the new product. For the instruction sessions offered during the implementation phase, participants can be informed about the upcoming changes. These individuals may also be good candidates for usability studies or focus groups conducted as part of the discovery interface rollout.

Gradual Acclimation

Early in the process of rolling out a new discovery interface the library can begin engaging the users. Because the product will serve as one of the library's prime end-user interfaces, it's important to take advantage of any possible opportunity to receive input from its target audience.

In Chapter 3, we considered a phased approach for launching the new discovery interface. These phases also form a part of the marketing effort. The early exposure of users to the product provides an awareness of the upcoming change as well as the new capabilities. Offering the product itself as a preview of what's to come later in the library's strategic search environment represents a powerful marketing approach. The progression of an early preview, followed by offering it as an alternate research interface, and finally presenting it as the standard search tool for the broader library collection should help drive use from its initial testing phase through operating at full capacity.

▶ MARKET THROUGH WEB POSITIONING

The success of the discovery product does not necessarily depend solely on publicity. While efforts of the kind described thus far may help build interest and support, the product must succeed on its own merits. If offered as the default search interface, users will find and use it. Determining how well it functions as a strategic information discovery platform or how well it's accepted is a matter for metrics and assessment (see Chapter 6). Although the act of placing the new discovery interface as the default search enforces a higher level of use, this by no means obviates the need to execute marketing and publicity. Those efforts help users understand the capabilities of the new interface, ease the transition, and contribute to a positive image of the library as offering interesting and powerful new services.

The single most important factor in increasing the use of the discovery interface is where it is positioned on the library's Web site. The vast majority of users of a Web site will follow the most obvious path to the task that they want to accomplish. If users intend to search for items in your collection, they will probably begin by typing in the first search box that they see, regardless of how it is labeled.

During the transition period prior to setting the new interface as the default search, the level of use that it receives will be determined largely by the relative placement of the two alternatives. If the online catalog stands out as the prominent search facility, it will be a challenge to attract sufficient numbers of users into the discovery interface in order to begin to expose it and to gain feedback. Likewise, if the new interface receives top billing and the traditional catalog is placed as the secondary, fall-back approach, the new interface can be expected to receive more use.

Once the project culminates with the placement of the discovery interface as the default search, its use should increase dramatically. As users visit the library's Web site with the intention of searching its collections, an unambiguous placement of the search box of the discovery interface will draw them in. As we will see in Chapter 6, a systematic approach to measuring and analyzing the use of the discovery interface will reveal its performance relative to the online catalog and other legacy search tools. The use levels of the discovery interface relative to that of the previous environment will indicate whether additional marketing and promotion is required.

Once the implementation of the discovery interface reaches completion, the library can adjust the focus of its marketing from this new resource to its broader Web presence. After it becomes the default search interface, its use levels should remain proportional to overall Web site activity. The problem at hand then shifts to driving interest and activity on the library's Web site to ever higher levels.

Once the library has modernized its Web presence through the introduction of a new discovery interface, likely in conjunction with other improvements, the library may want to launch a marketing campaign to entice potential users who may have been put off by the previous environment. In this later stage of marketing, the level of use of the discovery interface depends on the positioning of the library's Web site within the resources frequented by its patrons and on its discoverability through general Web search engines. For an academic library, it's vital to have visibility on the institutional Web site. The library should also be well placed within the course management system, virtual learning environments, and other Web-based systems frequented by its clientele.

▶ CONSIDER NAMING THE INTERFACE

When both the traditional catalog and the new discovery interface coexist, the relative use of the two may also be affected by the familiarity of an established name for the existing legacy catalog and some new name assigned to the discovery interface that users may not recognize. This issue also highlights the problem with assigning names to individual library products and services.

Many libraries assign names to their major services, especially to their catalogs. It's convenient to have a handle by which to refer to a resource that's complicated to describe. At Vanderbilt University, for example, we call our online catalog "Acorn," and this name has persisted through both of the ILSs we have used.

If the online catalog has a brand name, it raises questions about what to call the next-gen interface. Because the discovery interface works fundamentally different from the online catalog, many libraries do not want to give it the same name. Yet, coming up with a new name and getting it established will be difficult.

Establishing the recognition of a name associated with a given library service takes quite a bit of time and effort. Through consistent use by library personnel, on library Web sites, and through all the various elements of library communications, brand name will eventually stick. Users may not always understand the nuances of what they do, but named library catalogs often enjoy more brand recognition than the library itself. It might be argued that the branding effort should be reserved for the library itself and to simply use generic labels for specific products and services.

The ability to recycle the original name applied to the online catalog for the new discovery interface may also be affected by the planned disposition of the online catalog. Some libraries may plan to put the original catalog interface away entirely and position the discovery interface as a complete replacement. It's also common to position the discovery interface as the primary search tool but to preserve the online catalog as an advanced search option for the content managed within the ILS. The persistence of the original online catalog might generate confusion if the discovery interface takes its name. In such cases, a distinctive name for the discovery interface might be desired.

A related question involves the brand name associated with the search interface software or service. During the implementation process, it might be common to refer to the project or the service by the vendor's brand name. At some later point, the library will decide a name for its local implementation. It does not seem ideal for the library's name for the discovery interface to use the vendor's trade names or logos. While vendors may like the idea of greater exposure for their brands, it may add confusion to the library's own branding conventions. The license agreement may include statements regarding the vendor's brands or trademarks. Some agreements include a requirement for the company's trademark to appear on Web pages delivered by the interface. The default configuration of a discovery interface may include prominent use of the vendor's brands and logos.

As the library customizes the interface, it may need to make a conscious effort to remove this branding.

Whether the library decides to establish a brand name for its new discovery interface or use a generic name, once established the name should be used consistently in all communications. If the library makes a conscious effort during this early period, the name will become part of the library's ongoing vocabulary not only within the ranks of library personnel but also among its users. Leaving the naming issue unsettled or ambiguous may result in confusion. It's common, for example, for many libraries to refer to their ILS by the name of the company that produced it rather than the brand name of the software. This company name can even become associated with the online catalog. Taking on the brand names that companies use to market their products to libraries, or even using the name of the company to describe the product, can lead to confusion and does not help build and reinforce the brand of the library with its users.

▶ USE SEARCH WIDGETS FOR BRANDING

One of the important features of the new generation of discovery interfaces involves their ability to be positioned within applications external to the library. Libraries face the problem that many of its patrons do not think to visit the library as a discrete activity as they perform their research, choosing instead to use general Web search engines and other resources. The ability to insert library services directly into the course management system where students receive their assignments and reading lists is one example of how the discovery product can address the issue. It brings the library services to the user rather than relying on the user to visit the library, either virtually or physically.

Another way to bring library services to the user is to add a targeted search box to external resources. The use of widgets has become fairly well established. A search widget is a snippet of code that can be inserted in a Web resource that brings in the functionality of some other system. These widgets usually carry the branding of the service provided. OCLC, for example, offers a widget so that a WorldCat.org search can be embedded on a library Web site. Most of the publishers of information resources now provide widgets that can be used to embed search boxes, replete with their branding, on external pages. The search widgets from the companies that license content to libraries are becoming increasingly common on discipline-specific resource pages created by librarians, Web sites of academic departments, and on course pages. While it's helpful to provide a convenient way to search relevant resources from these locations, it's unfortunate that they carry the brands of library suppliers and not the libraries themselves.

A search widget associated with the discovery interface may address this problem in a way that better promotes and positions the library. If the discovery system can offer a search widget that can carry library brand and be programmed to filter queries according to the discipline at hand, this scenario would be a better solution than having to offer multiple search widgets associated with content suppliers. In the same way that a facet limits an existing search result when in the discovery interface, a search widget can apply the facet to the initial result set.

The ability to insert library-branded search widgets into external resources used by library patrons provides yet one more example of using the discovery interface as a tool for marketing the library.

► MARKET TO LIBRARY PERSONNEL

So far we have focused on marketing opportunities related to library users. It's also important to market the new discovery product to library personnel. I noted in Chapter 3 that it's important to build support for the project among the ranks of library staff members.

Depending on the size of the library, the market efforts directed at library personnel may be trivial or may require considerable attention. In small libraries, informal conversations among staff members may suffice. For large libraries, and especially for a consortium, the communications and marketing efforts to library staff need more careful planning and execution.

Throughout I have emphasized the importance of gaining buy-in from librarians and other library personnel. The success of the product for its intended end users may be impaired if the library staff don't support the product or are not well informed about its purpose or capabilities.

► EMPLOY SEARCH ENGINE OPTIMIZATION

One of the most powerful strategies for drawing users into an organization's Web presence involves optimizing the site for discovery through the major Internet search engines. The basic approach involves presenting the content of the site in such a way that it is easily harvested by the search engines, indexed, and assigned favorable position in results. This strategy, called Search Engine Optimization, or SEO, can make a major difference in the number of visitors to an organization's Web site.

A marketing strategy based on SEO recognizes that most library users may begin their research process in the general search engines. By paying attention to SEO techniques, the library can often attract its core clientele even when they begin with Google or one of its competitors.

It's vital to recognize the importance of search as a basic form of navigation on the Web. Users expect to simply type in the name of the site they want to view into the search box of their Web browser rather than depend on bookmarks or other structured lists. Given this dependence on search for navigation, it's essential that organizations, such as libraries, pay attention to their positioning in search engine results. At the very minimum, a library should ensure that it is listed first when a user types the library name into Google and other search engines. If the library's own Web site does not appear near the top of search engine results, it should perform an analysis of its Web site relative to the established practices of search engine optimization. Lack of attention to placing proper metadata within the headers and overly aggressive or devious SEO techniques can both lead to invisibility of the library's Web site in search engine results.

A more ambitious SEO strategy would involve leveraging the content of its unique collections to draw users into its Web presence. This approach involves presenting links to each item in the library's collection to the search engines in a way that they can be systematically harvested and indexed, and subsequently appear in search results.

This chapter has examined a variety of topics related to promoting the library's new discovery interface, including practical techniques and general ideas. I placed the topic at hand within the broader marketing and communications strategies and organizational structures that may already be in place. While I hope that these tips prove to be helpful, they should also be taken as suggestions to spark creative ideas from the reader.

▶5

BEST PRACTICES

> ▶ Maximize Discovery Interface Effectiveness
> ▶ Assemble a Toolkit

This book has so far given a great deal of practical advice related to the planning and implementation of a new discovery interface for your library. This chapter discusses some best practices to follow that will contribute to the success of the implementation project as well as provide broader benefits.

▶ MAXIMIZE DISCOVERY INTERFACE EFFECTIVENESS

Maintain high-quality metadata. To maximize the effectiveness of a discovery interface, all efforts must be made to ensure accurate and clean metadata. Next-gen products use metadata in ways considerably different from traditional catalogs. Issues not apparent in a legacy catalog may stand out when delivered through other environments. Improving the consistency and quality of metadata will return great benefits. Following good authority control procedures, for example, will improve the ability for a discovery interface to generate facets for navigation. Inconsistent forms of names and subject headings will result in facets that don't work quite right as users attempt to drill down to narrower search results. Clean data applies beyond the data extracted from the ILS. As the library populates the discovery interface with metadata from other resources, such as institutional repositories and digital collections, inconsistent application of metadata will cause problems. Efforts made toward clean and consistent metadata across all the resources that will be addressed by the discovery interface will yield improved search results and presentation for library users. One way to clean up metadata is to reconcile the library's bibliographic database with authority records. Such work can be performed by a bibliographic services firm or it can be handled internally. Libraries that have consistently maintained their bibliographic database with authority control will be ahead of the game.

The presence of a new discovery interface adds a new dimension to any project involving metadata. Many libraries, for example, take on projects to digitize photographs, manuscripts, and other kinds of materials. The digital representations created will likely be managed within a specialized environment that will include a metadata component. The metadata created for these projects should be designed not only for the needs of these specialized repositories but also for the discovery interface. A higher-level discovery interface brings the need to enforce standards in the way that metadata schemes are designed and how records are populated. Libraries involved in multiple digital projects especially need to be attentive to metadata issues. Most libraries would assent to these principles anyway. But it's when the data are actually contributed to a common environment, such as a discovery interface, that the degree to which they have been effective becomes known.

Aim for improvement, not perfection. The implementation of a new discovery interface should rank as but one step in the ongoing effort to modernize the library's Web presence. Don't wait for some perfect and final solution before moving forward with deliverables that will improve how patrons experience your library on the Web. It's often tempting to defer action until an ideal product might emerge, despite substantial levels of dissatisfaction with the status quo. We've not yet seen the last and final products in this genre. The current slate is evolving rapidly, and surely new products will come on the scene. Waiting for "the market to mature" may be a safe approach, but it runs counter to a strategy of continuous incremental improvement.

Circumstances vary, of course, from library to library, but for many libraries, launching a product in the short term that effects substantial improvement will make more sense than holding back a year for a more refined approach. It's only when the library turns on the new product to its full user base that it sees the full impact of its strengths and flaws. Of course, the launch of a new discovery interface should involve every effort to create the best service possible, but don't get caught up in endless rounds of internal testing before taking the plunge to see how your users actually approach your new offering. If your library already feels the rumblings of discontent from users regarding the legacy catalog and other information delivery tools, then the urgency for change may outweigh the desire to take a slower more deliberate approach.

Use cascading style sheets for consistency of presentation. A good Web site will exhibit consistency in look and feel throughout. The discovery interface needs to fit within the library's broader Web presence. Visitors should not see jarring differences in the look of the pages as they navigate from the initial Web site into the discovery interface. All of the components within the library's Web site should use the same color scheme, logos, page banners, footers, and navigation elements to the extent possible. Cascading style sheets (CSS) provide a powerful mechanism for the control of presentation.

Web applications should separate content and structure from presentation. This approach involves generating HTML with very basic tags, avoiding any hard-coding of presentation features. Font selection, size, colors, and even page layout should be left out of HTML coding and left to directives specified in an accompanying CSS. In an application such as a discovery interface, the library may have little control over the way that it generates each page presented to the user. But to the extent that these applications use CSS, it becomes possible to develop style sheets that can be shared among applications or at least managed in a way that the library can execute its presentation preferences through similar coding in each application's style sheets.

Insist on perfect pages. It's vital to insist that every Web page generated within your Web presence, including and especially the discovery interface, embody valid, standards-compliant HTML. Much of the HTML will be programmatically generated and not necessarily under the control of the library. Part of the testing of the discovery interface should include the validation of each kind of page it delivers. If validation problems persist, the library may need to work with the vendor to address this issue. Valid HTML is vital to ensure predictable performance, especially across a variety of Web browsers.

▶ ASSEMBLE A TOOLKIT

The process of implementing a discovery interface involves a variety of components that can be applied to other projects, such as the ancillary technical utilities that extract and manipulate the metadata. When creating these utilities, strive for the most generalized approach so that it can be used beyond the task at hand. Other reusable assets involve the skills and knowledge of the personnel participating in the project. The expertise developed during the initial implementation of the discovery interface should find many future applications. Especially in the vein of continuous improvement and enhancement of the discovery interface and other aspects of the library's Web presence, these skills will find ample opportunity for exercise. The discovery interface project should improve the skills and heighten the awareness of library personnel in a variety of ways that will benefit the library in this crucial area of information delivery.

Implementing a new discovery interface is a multidisciplinary endeavor. The project involves an intersection of many different kinds of library personnel. While it's obvious that technical staff and project managers will be involved, metadata specialists and others who deliver services to the public should often be firmly engaged. As these groups cross-pollinate their expertise, experience, and perspectives, the project will benefit both directly in implementation details and indirectly in process issues, yielding improved buy-in. Naturally, this cross-disciplinary approach shouldn't be confined to the planning and implementation period but should be part of the ongoing processes of evaluation and improvement of the library's virtual facilities as well.

Look to the future. As the library works toward the completion of a new discovery interface, it's time to start thinking about what to do next. This genre of products is evolving rapidly, with major revisions in technology underway and especially in the creation and expansion of indexes to provide access to more article collections. When it comes to the products that involve the library's Web presence, there's little time for complacency. Maintaining a cutting-edge Web presence requires ongoing diligence.

►6

MEASURES OF SUCCESS

- ► **Assess Benchmark Patterns and Trends**
- ► **Use Measurement and Analysis Tools**
- ► **Monitor Subscription-Based Resources**
- ► **Measure the Impact of Discovery**

I have emphasized the importance of the library's Web presence as a vehicle for the delivery of library content and services. To understand its own performance, a library needs to continually monitor the use of each of the components of its environment. Libraries can employ any of a variety of tools and techniques to measure and analyze use. This chapter provides a few basic suggestions that libraries can extend or expand upon to support their specific assessment needs.

The implementation of a new discovery interface is a major project that will consume a portion of a library's time, energy, and budget. An analysis of usage data can help reveal the need for a new approach to providing access to the collections and may provide some of the evidence needed to justify the allocation of resources. Usage data are a valuable resource to support decision making. Attention to collecting and analyzing such data will be useful not only for a project to implement a new discovery interface but also any project involving any of the components of a library's Web-based services. Many libraries embrace the value of assessment and continually monitor the performance of each aspect of their services and collections.

It's never too early to begin systematically measuring the use of the library's virtual environment. If you don't start during the planning and early implementation phases of a project, such as a new discovery interface, it will be impossible to measure the impact of the product because you won't have data that benchmark existing usage levels and patterns.

▶ ASSESS BENCHMARK PATTERNS AND TRENDS

To assess the impact of any change made to the library's Web environment, it's essential to have a good understanding of what constitutes normal use for any given period. Any Web site will exhibit fluctuations in activity levels. The analysis of the impact of a change must take into consideration the context of usage pattern cycles. In general, the measure of the impact of a change must be made by measuring use across comparable cycles. Each library will have its distinctive seasonal, weekly, and even daily usage patterns.

Academic and school libraries tend to have the most dramatic patterns given their ties to the academic calendar and the lifestyle of students. The cycles of use in public libraries tend to be more subtle but are still subject to regular patterns of variation. Regardless of type, libraries should visualize their normal use patterns and be on guard for unexpected deviations.

One of the most commonly studied pattern is the **weekly** pattern. For many of the sites I monitor, highest use occurs on Mondays, decreasing each day through Saturday, with a rise on Sunday, peaking again on the next Monday (see Figure 6.1).

Seasonal patterns are pertinent to a number of libraries. Academic libraries will naturally observe that usage patterns vary according to the academic year. We generally expect higher use when classes are in session and significantly lower use during break periods. We also expect peak use toward the end of each session. Periods when students actively work on papers and projects involve higher use than exam times. The graph in Figure 6.2 illustrates the typical seasonal use pattern of an academic library. Levels are lower during summer months, and activity builds throughout a semester, with dramatic dips for major academic holidays such as winter and spring breaks.

It's also helpful to understand the ebbs and flows of **daily** (and nighttime) use. Typical patterns show heaviest use mid-day, with moderate levels continuing through the evening, trailing off in the early morning. Daily patterns may change considerably during periods of intensive study, such as when papers come due at the end of a class session (see Figure 6.3).

Retention of Data

In today's environment of abundant storage, it's feasible to keep detailed statistics reflecting past use indefinitely. Libraries, given our pri-

▶ Figure 6.1: Typical Weekly Usage Fluctuations of a Library Web Site

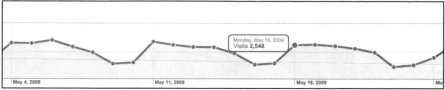

▶ Figure 6.2: Typical Seasonal Usage Fluctuations of a Library Web Site

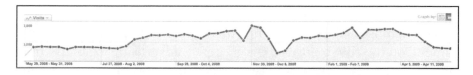

▶ Figure 6.3: Typical Daily Usage Fluctuations of a Library Web Site

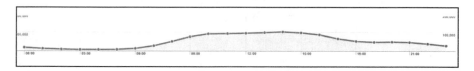

ority to preserve the privacy of our users, will likely want to strip away any fields that contain data that identify specific individuals. Once safely sanitized, these log files will remain valuable for any studies that the library conducts that involve historic usage patterns.

▶ USE MEASUREMENT AND ANALYSIS TOOLS

Libraries can use a variety of tools to measure and analyze the use of their Web site. The cost ranges from free on up to tens of thousands of dollars, and the sophistication levels vary. Be aware that the costs aren't necessarily proportional to the levels of sophistication. Some of the tools available without cost have excellent capabilities.

"Web analytics" is the genre of software designed to analyze the use of Web servers, generating many different graphs and reports that characterize overall levels and patterns of use. These applications base their analysis on raw data registered by the Web server each time it responds to a request. These raw use data are created in different ways. Some Web servers record each request in a log file that they store in a standard format as a file on the server. These log files are then processed by a Web analytics package, which often includes converting log entries into database records for increased flexibility in producing reports according to specific data ranges and categories. These Web analytics base their analyses on Web server logs:

- ▶ AWStats, an open source log analyzer, available at http://awstats .sourceforge.net
- ▶ Unica Web Analytics, available at http://netinsight.unica.com
- ▶ SawMill, available in Lite, Professional, and Enterprise versions at www.sawmill.net

The commercial Web analytics products target corporations that depend on their Web sites for e-commerce, advertising, or marketing, offering features that help these organizations optimize the generation of revenue. The costs of some of the high-end analytics packages may be out of the reach of many libraries.

Another technique for Web analytics, often called "page tagging," relies on transmitting usage data to an external repository for later reporting and analysis. Page tagging eliminates the need for access to server logs, which may be a problem for many Web sites. To use a page tagging analytics, each page needs to execute a small JavaScript program to convey data to the repository each time it is requested.

Google Analytics, one of the most popular Web analytics tools, relies on page tagging. Available without cost simply by registering for an account, Google Analytics includes a set of reports and graphs that should meet the needs of most libraries (see Figure 6.4). Getting started with Google Analytics involves setting up a profile for each Web site and generating the code that needs to be inserted on each page. On most Web sites, it should be possible to add this snippet of JavaScript to a global page footer, which avoids the need to manually edit each page. Once the snippet has been activated, usage data begin to accumulate. Reports can be generated for any subsequent period. This approach does not allow you to produce reports on historic data prior to the inclusion of the page tagging snippet. Reports from earlier times will need to be created with a Web analytics utility based on Web server logs, provided that these logs have been preserved.

One of the key characteristics of Google Analytics is the transmission of usage data to Google servers. The process does not transmit data that personally identify users, but libraries will need to consider

▶ Figure 6.4: Google Analytics Dashboard (www.google.com/analytics) Summarizing Web Site Use

whether this model raises concern regarding their policies of patron privacy.

Web analytics tools can be used not only for the library's basic Web site but for all of its Web-based resources. A library will want to pay close attention to the use of its online catalog, discovery interface, digital library products, institutional repositories, and all other Web-based components of its overall Web presence. As long as it's possible to gain access to the server logs or have the ability to add the page tagging code, any of these applications can be monitored through Web analytics software.

Many Web-based applications also generate their own internal utilities for monitoring and reporting use. These utilities can provide information difficult to derive through general Web analytics, such as data related to types of users and specific interactions with content resources. When considering the use of a Web-based application that has internal usage reporting capabilities, it's often interesting and helpful to compare these results with those compiled by general Web analytics. Similar findings will confirm that the results represent actual use. Any differences can be explored to better understand which tool presents the more reliable reflection of use. Multiple tools often complement each other in the way that they describe use.

► MONITOR SUBSCRIPTION-BASED RESOURCES

The methods described thus far do not have the ability to measure the use of some content resources and services provided externally. Electronic journals, databases, and other content resources to which the library subscribes do not fall within the realm of what can be measured through Web analytics. Yet, it's critical to have usage data for each of these resources by a library's clientele to inform collection decisions on the relative value of each resource. Libraries especially need detailed data to inform their decisions about which products to subscribe to on a trial basis and which of their existing subscriptions to renew or terminate.

Libraries depend mostly on statistics provided by their electronic resources publishers and vendors to know how they have been access by their users. It is very difficult for a library to produce its own definitive statistics regarding the use of the electronic resources to which they subscribe. While it's possible to count the click-throughs on the links that the library provides to each resource, many users bypass the library's environment and access their favorite resources directly. Libraries have developed a standard format, called COUNTER (Counting Online Usage of Networked Electronic Resources), for the delivery of publisher-provided statistics. In recent years SUSHI (Standardized Usage Statistics Harvesting Initiative) has become a widely accepted automatic mechanism for providing COUNTER-compliant statistics. COUNTER and SUSHI are the primary tools for gathering data on electronic resources. These usage statistics can then be loaded into spreadsheets or electronic resource management systems for analysis.

► MEASURE THE IMPACT OF DISCOVERY

To get a sense of the impact of a project, the library will want to consider a wide variety of metrics. While it's interesting to know about the level of use of the discovery interface itself, it's the changes in usage patterns across the broader environment of library resources that portrays the true picture of the impact brought about by a new discovery interface.

The use of electronic resources may be affected not only by the quality of the content and its suitability to research needs but also by the degree of difficulty that users experience in finding it or in learning that it's available to them. One of the primary goals of a discovery interface lies in guiding users to library-provided resources that they have not otherwise experienced.

Discovery Interface Usage Levels

One basic metric that indicates the success of the discovery interface is the activity levels of the application itself. The overall activity of the discovery interface points to the level of engagement. Usage statistics lower than anticipated may indicate a problem with the flow of the Web site relative to guiding the users into the search box of the discovery interface.

If your library offers both a new discovery interface and the original online catalog, you want to investigate the usage levels of both, as well as the combined total. Does use of the discovery interface come at the expense of the online catalog, or is there an increased amount of search activity overall?

Explore the internal usage reporting of the discovery interface, and become familiar with the methods used for counting unique visitors, the sessions, and transactions per session. The discovery interface may also provide data regarding the types of searches selected, counts of facets or filters invoked, full records displayed, and some measure of the frequency that the interface successfully connects the user to a resource.

When possible, use multiple tools to measure the activity of the Web-based resources, such as a Web analytics utility in addition to the internal reporting capabilities of the discovery interface. For example, register the discovery interface with Google Analytics and add the page tagging code to the templates used to define layout. Once configured, confirm that both tools report similar levels of use, at least regarding the number of sessions and other measures of general activity. If large discrepancies exist, explore the measuring techniques that both utilities employ to ensure that they extract comparable statistics. Consistency between the internal usage report of the discovery interface and that of general Web analytics will build confidence that the two measures accurately reflect use.

It may be difficult, however, to ensure consistent usage metrics between the old and new environments. The usage and navigation patterns of the new interface will differ from those of online catalogs. We would expect differences in the overall proportions of sessions, search operations, and discrete pages viewed of an interface based on faceted navigation compared to traditional online catalogs.

Another interesting usage question concerns search efficiency. How many pages does the interface have to deliver to achieve a successful search result? A smaller number of pages per session might be interpreted as a positive indicator. A more detailed approach might involve following individual search sessions, to determine which ones appear to conclude with a successful outcome versus those that did not yield satisfactory results.

Legacy Catalog versus Discovery Interface Usage Levels

One interesting set of metrics will compare the usage levels of the new discovery interface with that of the online catalog. During transitional periods when the library offers both the online catalog and the discovery interface, usage statistics will reveal the proportion of searching done under each platform. Interpret the differences cautiously. Higher use of one platform over the other may have as much to do with how they are positioned on the Web site as with user preferences. When presented with multiple search options, users may, for example, choose the one with which they are familiar rather than explore a new alternative.

Once the library positions the new discovery interface as the default search, it will be of interest to compare its use levels with those of its predecessor. One would hope that the introduction of a more successful interface would result in more interest by library patrons as reflected in higher usage statistics, and this should be confirmed empirically. An increase should be expected and taken as a marker of success. Hopefully, a more modern tool will seem more engaging to library users.

Changing Dynamics of the Library's Overall Web Presence

We've noted throughout that many of the discovery interfaces address a broader scope of content than the traditional online catalog, especially with regard to e-journals and other electronic and digital content. Note whether the usage statistics confirm changes in the way that users gain access to the various components of the library's collections. If the discovery interface successfully connects users with e-journal content, expect to see not only an increase in the use of the discovery interface over the previous online catalog but also a decrease in use of the traditional set of search tools associated with the library's e-journal collections. In other words, if the new discovery interface is positioned as the all-in-one search tool, its usage statistics should reflect a total level of activity that is at least equivalent to the online catalog plus that of the tools used to access electronic resources.

By using a variety of tools applied across each of the applications and resources within the library's Web presence, it becomes possible to understand the dynamics of the site and what kinds of change the new tool made. It should be possible to see whether aggregate activity across the entire Web presence has increased or not, whether the number of combined searches has changed, and especially the impact on the number of resources retrieved or viewed.

Impact on the Physical Collection

We've noted that the legacy online catalogs tend to specialize in the physical inventory of the library at the expense of adequate treatment of electronic content. As you shift to a discovery interface, you will want to know whether users continue to find the print material as easily as before. To gauge the ability of the discovery interface to provide adequate access to the physical resources, look for significant changes in the following:

▶ Circulation statistics
▶ Interlibrary loan requests
▶ Branch transfers
▶ Direct consortial borrowing systems

Impact on the Electronic Collection

I noted earlier in this chapter that publishers and providers of e-journals, databases, and other subscription-based electronic content provide detailed usage statistics to libraries through COUNTER and SUSHI. If one of the key goals of the discovery interface involves improving access to the library's overall collection, any changes in the usage levels of electronic resources should be noteworthy. These questions will help you measure such changes:

▶ Has the aggregate use of electronic resources increased subsequent to the introduction of the discovery interface?
▶ Has the new interface led to any change in the usage patterns of electronic resources? For example, were there previously patterns of high use clustered around a few high-profile resources? Did the discovery interface result in a different distribution in use across resources?

> ▶ Are there some resources that have seen increases or decreases in use that might have resulted from the change in the discovery environment?
>
> ▶ Did the introduction of the discovery environment result in increased use of high-quality resources that were previously underused?

Some libraries view a new discovery interface as a tool to expose users to information resources otherwise neglected. In today's tough economic climate, it's hard to justify expensive electronic resources that don't receive adequate use, even when they have excellent content. A successful discovery interface should offer some help in guiding users to these resources by including their content with appropriate relevance ranking in results lists. The library may be able to effect some differences in the relative use of its resource by fine-tuning the relevance weighting and positioning within its discovery environment. This kind of tweaking cannot be accomplished without measurement and analysis of use prior to and following changes made within the discovery environment.

The correlation between the introduction of the discovery interface and changes in the use of resources is affected by other factors as well. Most libraries have experienced an increased use of electronic resources over time. Does the introduction of the discovery interface account for changes that would not have happened anyway or that can be explained by normal fluctuations throughout the academic or calendar year?

Differences may not be immediate or measureable within short periods of time. When performing a comparative analysis, it may be necessary to look at many different periods in order to understand the total impact of a change. Data from the same point in the previous academic calendar year provides an interesting point of comparison. Shorter-term comparisons can also be helpful provided that you factor out other expected changes. If, for example, you introduce a change in the third week of an academic semester and notice a significant increase in the use of a targeted resource in the fifth week, it would be important to know if such an increase was part of a seasonal pattern noted in previous years or whether it was beyond historic trends. If the normal pattern of use between the fourth and fifth week was typically a 10 percent increase and you saw a 30 percent rise, it would confirm a positive change.

These questions illustrate some of the kinds of changes that library staff should consider as they assess the impact of the new discovery interface on the use of library resources. In some cases an informal review of the usage statistics will reveal patterns that confirm success. Libraries that need a more detailed assessment can perform a formal statistical analysis.

▶

REFERENCES AND RELATED RESOURCES

Much of the content included here is available in open access through the author's Library Technology Guides Web site (www.librarytechnology .org).

Bowen, Jennifer. 2008. "Metadata to Support Next-Generation Library Resource Discovery: Lessons from the eXtensible Catalog, Phase 1." *Information Technology and Libraries* 27, no. 2 (June): 6–20. An early progress report on the eXtensible Catalog project that focuses on the way that the interface will manage and improve metadata to enhance the discovery process.

Breeding, Marshall. 2002. "The Open Archives Initiative." *Information Today* 19, no. 4 (April): 46–47. The protocol used by most discovery interfaces emerged out of the Open Archives Initiative. This article provides some background information that explains advantages of the metadata harvesting approach over other federated search methods.

———. 2002. "Understanding the Protocol for Metadata Harvesting of the Open Archives Initiative." *Computers in Libraries* 22, no. 8 (September): 24–29. This article introduces the OAI-PMH protocol and provides some technical details on how it functions.

———. 2005. "Plotting a New Course for Metasearch." *Computers in Libraries* 25, no. 2 (February): 27–30. In this edition of the "Systems Librarian" column, Breeding talks about the advantages of centralized search models such as OAI-PMH over distributed search.

———. 2007. "The Birth of a New Generation of Library Interfaces." *Computers in Libraries* 27, no. 9 (October): 34–37. This "Systems Librarian" column describes some of the features and concepts coalescing in the emerging genre of discovery interfaces.

———. 2007. "Building the eXtensible Catalog." ALA TechSource. *Smart Libraries Newsletter* 27, no. 112 (December): 3. A news article that introduces the eXtensible Catalog project at the University of Rochester River Campus Libraries and reports on its progress.

————. 2007. "Next-Generation Library Catalogs." ALA TechSource. *Library Technology Reports* 43, no. 4 (July/August). This issue of *Library Technology Reports* provides an introduction to the emerging genre of new library interfaces and analyzes each of the products that were available at that time.

————. 2007. "VuFind: A Next-Generation Catalog from Villanova." ALA TechSource. *Smart Libraries Newsletter* 27, no 9 (September): 1. This news article describes the open source development project out of the Villanova University Libraries to create a discovery interface based on Apache Lucene and SOLR.

————. 2008. "Beyond the Current Generation of Next-Generation Library Interfaces: Deeper Search." *Computers in Libraries* 28, no. 5 (May): 39–42. In this "Systems Librarian" column, Breeding talks about the importance of taking advantage of the full text of resources for discovery and the advantages of this approach over indexes created solely from bibliographic records or citation data.

————. 2008. "The Library Corporation Works toward a New ILS Platform." *Smart Libraries Newsletter* 28, no. 12 (December): 4–5. This news article reports on the new LS2 PAC catalog interface developed by The Library Corporation and the company's efforts to build an entirely new integrated library system on this platform.

————. 2008. "Progress on the DLF ILS Discovery Interface API: The Berkeley Accord." National Standards Information Organization. *Information Standards Quarterly* (Summer): 18–19. Based on the author's participation in the meetings held at the University of California in Berkeley, the report summarizes the specifications of the ILS Discovery Interface API and provides an update on the participants' intentions regarding the proposals.

————. 2008. "SirsiDynix Launches Its Faceted Search Product." ALA TechSource. *Smart Libraries Newsletter* (August): 3. This news article reports on Enterprise, the faceted search interface developed by SirsiDynix using the Brainware search technology.

————. 2009. "OCLC Partners with EBSCO to Expand Access to Articles in WorldCat Local." *Smart Libraries Newsletter* 29, no. 5 (May): 1–4. This news article describes developments regarding the partnership between EBSCO Information Services and OCLC to provide article-level citation records for WorldCat Local.

————. 2009. "Open Source Discovery Interfaces Gain Momentum." *Smart Libraries Newsletter* 29, no. 4 (April): 1–4. This news article describes the current status of some of the open source discovery interface projects such as VuFind and Blacklight and some of the library organizations adopting them.

————. 2009. "Summon: A New Search Service from Serials Solutions." *Smart Libraries Newsletter* 29, no. 3 (March): 1–3. This feature article introduces the new Summon discovery service and describes the approach that Serials Solutions used to create its massive index of article-level content and local content derived from the ILS and other information repositories.

Calhoun, Karen. 2006. "The Changing Nature of the Catalog and Its Integration with Other Discovery Tools." Report prepared for the Library of Congress, March 17, 2006. Available: www.loc.gov/catdir/calhoun-report -final.pdf (accessed December 20, 2009). This seminal report commissioned by the Library of Congress has been widely discussed in conversations involving how libraries should organize their cataloging and metadata operations. The report relates to library discovery interfaces in that it addresses issues related to the metadata, for both print and digital resources, that populate these tools.

Calhoun, Karen, Joanne Cantrell, Peggy Gallaher, and Janet Hawk. 2009. "Online Catalogs: What Users and Librarians Want." Available: www.oclc .org/reports/onlinecatalogs/fullreport.pdf (accessed December 20, 2009). This 68-page report provides an extensive look into the expectations of library users for online library catalogs and how they differ in some ways from the requirements of librarians.

Camden, Beth Picknally. 2008. "OPAC—Going, Going, Gone!" *Technicalities* 28, no. 5 (Sept/Oct): 1–4. The author describes some of the shortcomings of the traditional online library catalog and how some of the successors, such as WorldCat Local, address some of these concerns. Open source projects such as PennTags, VuFind, BlackLight, and the eXtensible Catalog have emerged to meet local needs not resolved by commercial projects.

Dempsey, Lorcan. 2008. "Reconfiguring the Library Systems Environment" (Guest Editorial). *portal: Libraries and the Academy* 8, no. 2: 111–120. This essay written by the VP and Chief Strategist of OCLC explores some of the ways that the traditional library automation and discovery systems might be reconsidered in light of the changed realities in the ways that libraries manage content and the expectations of library users.

———. 2009. "Metasearch Redux." Available: http://orweblog.oclc.org/ archives/001933.html (accessed December 20, 2009).

Fifarek, Aimee. 2007. "The Birth of Catalog 2.0: Innovative Interfaces' Encore Discovery Platform." *Library Hi-Tech News* 24, no. 5 (May): 13. The author provides a detailed description of Encore and the ways that it implements Web 2.0 concepts as a next-generation library catalog.

Kaizer, Jasper and Anthony Hodge. 2005. "AquaBrowser Library: Search, Discover, Refine." *Library Hi-Tech News* 25, no. 10: 9–12. Authored by two individuals from Medialab Solutions, the developers of the product, this article describes the features of the AquaBrowser Library discovery interface and the search technologies it employs.

Katz-Haas, Raïssa and Aimée Truchard, eds. 1998. "Usability Techniques: Ten Guidelines for User-Centered Web Design." *Usability Interface* 5, no. 1 (July). Available: www.stcsig.org/usability/newsletter/9807-webguide.html

(accessed December 20, 2009). This Web-based resource provides ten very practical guidelines based on the principles of user-centered design as an organization develops or redesigns its Web site.

Lindström, Henrik and Martin Malmsten. 2008. "User-Centered Design and the Next-Generation OPAC—A Perfect Match?" Presentation delivered at the 32nd Library Systems Seminar, European Libraries Automation Group 2008 Conference. Wageningen, the Netherlands, April 16, 2008. Available: http://library.wur.nl/elag2008/presentations/Lindstrom_ Malmsten.pdf (accessed December 20, 2009). This paper describes the process of user-centered design employed by the National Library of Sweden as it developed the next generation interface for the Swedish National Union Catalog.

Marcin, Susan and Peter Morris. 2008. "OPAC: The Next Generation: Placing an Encore Front End onto a SirsiDynix ILS." *Computers in Libraries* 28, no. 5 (May): 6–9, 62–64. This article describes the efforts of the library at Fairfield University to implement the Encore discovery interface from Innovative Interfaces with the Unicorn ILS from SirsiDynix.

Mayfield, Ian, Linda Humphres, Steve Shadle, and Morag Watson. 2008. "Next- Generation Library Catalogs: Reviews of ELIN, WorldCat Local and AquaBrowser." *Serials* 21, no. 3 (November): 224–230. This article includes sections that provide basic descriptions and reviews of three discovery interfaces.

McClure, Randall and Kellian Clink. 2009. "How Do You Know That? An Investigation of Student Research Practices in the Digital Age." *portal: Libraries and the Academy* 9, no. 1 (January): 115–132. The authors investigate the ways that undergraduate English composition students use sources for assigned course essays with some analysis of the quality of those sources, primarily those found online.

Medeiros, Norm. 1999. "Driving with Eyes Closed: The Perils of Traditional Catalogs and Cataloging in the Internet Age" *Library Computing* 18, no. 4: 300–306. This article, written a decade ago, provides a critique of cataloging processes that focus too narrowly on traditional print resources in an age where electronic information on the Internet increasingly dominates.

Next Generation Catalog Interest Group. LITA (Library & Information Technology Association). Available: www.ala.org/ala/mgrps/divs/lita/litamembership/litaigs/nextgencatalog/nextgencatalog.cfm (accessed December 20, 2009). The Web site of this special interest group of LITA devoted to next-generation catalogs provides current information on meetings, programs, officers, and relevant resources.

NGC4LIB (Next Generation Catalogs for Libraries) Discussion List. Available: http://serials.infomotions.com/ngc4lib (accessed December 20, 2009). This discussion list, managed by Eric Lease Morgan of Notre Dame University, focuses on issues related to next-generation discovery interfaces. The Web site for the list provides a search interface for the archives of the list's messages.

River Campus Libraries, University of Rochester. 2009. "Extensible Catalog (XC)." Available: www.extensiblecatalog.org (accessed May 25, 2009). This Web site describes an effort funded by the Andrew W. Mellon Foundation to study how best to develop a next- generation catalog in an open-source model.

Rochkind, Jonathan. 2007. "(Meta)search Like Google." *Library Journal* (February 15). Available: www.libraryjournal.com/article/CA6413442.html (accessed December 20, 2009). This article discusses the benefits of acquiring full-text content from the publishers of information resources to create large Google-like indexes of library content. The article describes some of the problems associated with metasearch based on simultaneous live search connections.

Ruschoff, Carlen. 2008. "The Integrated Library System: Are You Ready for the Next Generation ILS?" *Technicalities* 28, no. 6 (Nov/ Dec): 1–4.

Sokvitne, Lloyd. "Redesigning the OPAC: Moving Outside of the IMLS." State Library of Tasmania. Available: www.alia.org.au/publishing/aarl/37.4/sokvitne.pdf (accessed December 20, 2009). This article describes some of the concepts of a next-generation library catalog and the project carried out at the State Library of Tasmania to create a new search interface with faceted navigation using the Verity search engine.

Ward, Jennifer L., Steve Shadle, and Pam Mofjeld. 2009. "WorldCat Local at the Univ. of Washington Libraries." *Library Technology Reports* 44, no. 6. This issue of *Library Technology Reports* describes various aspects of WorldCat Local and its implementation at the University of Washington Libraries. The issue provides a detailed look at the architecture and technology involved in WorldCat Local and the experiences of one of the pilot libraries that implemented it.

INDEX

Page numbers followed by the letter "t" indicate tables.